A GARDENER'S GUIDE TO

Organic gardening

EDITOR VALERIE DUNCAN
SERIES EDITOR GRAHAM STRONG

MEREHURST

Merehurst Ltd, Ferry House, 51-57 Lacy Road, Putney, London SW15 1PR

CONTENTS

WHAT IS ORGANIC GARDENING?

ORGANIC GARDENING IS NOTHING MORE
THAN THE APPLICATION OF COMMON SENSE

Not so long ago, most gardeners regarded organic gardening as the preserve of eccentrics who refused to accept the self-evident truth that twentieth-century progress had transformed the ancient art of gardening. Why fiddle around with compost and marigolds when modern fertilizers and insecticides were so much more efficient and easier to use?

Opinions have changed, and now many gardeners regard 'organic' as the most sensible way to garden. For the benefits of twentieth-century technology came at a price: chemical sprays and fertilizers have done much damage to the environment. We might not think that we can do much to change the world, but we can take sensible care of the one part of the environment we do control: our own garden. And by doing so, we make a difference. Add up all the gardens in the country and they represent a large chunk of its environment.

But it is unwise to see organic gardening as just a catalogue of negative commandments: do not use chemical fertilizers, poisonous insecticides, weed-killers and so on. Organic gardening is a positive way of working in harmony with nature, for example, by feeding the soil, creating diversity, recycling or simply growing the right plant in the right place. Think of organic gardening more as the application of the simple common sense that gardeners have been practising for centuries.

Have you ever dug manure into a planting bed? Put kitchen scraps on a compost heap? Used blood, fish and bone to encourage the tomatoes rather than, say, sulphate of ammonia? Turned a strong jet from the hose on the rose bushes to drown the aphids instead of reaching for a poison spray? If you have, then you have been practising organic gardening, probably without giving it a second thought.

Organic gardening is not so very different from conventional gardening – tomatoes are still planted in spring, roses pruned in winter, the lawn (alas!) still has to be mowed and fertilizer and pest controls still need to be applied from time to time. But there is a special satisfaction to be gained when you spread, not a bag of chemical fertilizer from the garden centre, but a rich, home-made compost. You know that it will benefit not just the immediate growth of your plants but the health of the soil for years to come. This is working hand in hand with Nature, in harmony with her own rhythms.

An organic garden arranged in an attractive, informal style, with tomatoes and rows of lettuce mingling with cosmos, gladiolus and dahlia. While not strictly ordered, this style of garden is still pleasing to the eye and provides a flourishing and diverse plant community. The immediate growth of the plants as well as the health of the soil will benefit if you practise organic gardening.

THE BEAUTIFUL ORGANIC
GARDEN

AN ORGANIC GARDEN CAN BE AS
BEAUTIFUL AS ANY OTHER GARDEN

Many people first develop an enthusiasm for organic gardening because they want to grow vegetables and fruit that are free from chemical contamination. However, the principles of organic gardening are just as important in the decorative garden, and the ornamental garden is an essential part of the organic garden as a whole. There is very little point in

Red lupins mingle with other flowers in a garden border. Lupins are legumes and are useful additions to any ornamental garden as they add nitrogen to the soil, as well as being decorative.

nurturing an organic vegetable garden if you are then going to spray the flower garden with herbicides and insecticides which could contaminate a much wider area and disrupt the balance of nature in the garden overall.

For some people organic gardening conjures up images of a weedy wilderness, but there is no reason why this should be the case. Organic gardening is a philosophy and method of gardening, rather than a style of gardening, and it is possible to apply the principles of organic gardening to create a beautiful garden of any type, formal or informal, large or small, productive or purely decorative. Although you can grow the same types of plants as in a non-organic garden, it may be better to choose varieties that are more vigorous or disease resistant, and you may need to be more careful in placing them.

When planning ornamental borders, the aim, as well as the aesthetic one of designing a garden that gives you a beautiful and pleasing environment to enjoy, is to create a diverse plant community that will flourish throughout the year. This will provide a means of attracting a wide range of beneficial wildlife to the garden – from insects and birds to

The beautiful colours of Cosmos, *lupins and lavender mingle in a decorative organic garden, demonstrating that the principles of organic gardening can also be applied to the ornamental garden. By creating a diverse community of plantlife you will gain colour and interest, as well as provide food and shelter for wildlife, in a garden that can be enjoyed all year round.*

small mammals – and help create the balanced environment that enables an organic garden to thrive without the addition of artificial chemicals.

Although any style of garden can be maintained organically if well planned, the cottage garden style, in which shrubs, perennials, bulbs, annuals and even herbs and vegetables mingle in an informal manner, is ideal for creating this type of balanced community and ensuring that no pest or disease is likely to get the upper hand.

Choose a variety of plants that will give you colour and interest and provide food and shelter for wildlife over as long a season as possible. While virtually all flowers will provide nectar and pollen for insects, there are some that are particularly attractive to beneficial insects, such as bees and hoverflies. It is worth searching out some of these plants and including a range that will provide

flowers throughout as much of the year as possible. Not only will the wildlife benefit but you will enjoy the array of flowers as well.

Try, too, to select a range of plants that will give extra value with more than one season of interest, such as those with colourful berries in autumn as well as flowers in the spring, plants with beautiful scents, or those that make good ground cover or have colourful or evergreen foliage.

A major key to success in the organic garden is simply to grow the right plants in the right place. By working with nature, and giving your plants the conditions they need and will naturally flourish in, instead of trying to maintain them in conditions that are at the edge of their range of tolerance, they will be vigorous, healthy and much better able to shrug off attacks by pests and diseases. They will give you a much better display as well.

ABOVE: *A beehive nestles next to a blackcurrant bush and a rich mixture of flowers in this flourishing cottage garden border. The cottage garden style is not only widely appreciated, but is also a style that is well-suited to the basic principles of organic gardening as it creates a varied and balanced plant community.*
LEFT: *A closer view of an attractive cottage garden border where* Eschscholzia, Nemophila *and* Phacelia *mingle in a superb display of colourful informality.*

ABOVE: *Even a vegetable garden need not be unattractive. In this cottage garden potager the neatly raised beds of vegetables and herbs are surrounded by a mixture of flowers in tubs and borders. The principles of organic gardening are just as relevant to the flower garden as to the vegetable garden. There is little point in nurturing an organic vegetable garden if you are then going to spray the flower garden with herbicides and insecticides which could contaminate a much wider area and disrupt the natural balance.*

LEFT: *Mounds of geraniums, poppies,* Cistus *and* Potentilla *flourish in this informal border. A mulch of gravel not only makes an attractive background for the plants but it also reduces the need for watering and is effective in suppressing weed growth.*

GROWING FLOWERS
ORGANICALLY

BEAUTIFUL FLOWERS CAN BE GROWN ORGANICALLY,
WHICH WILL ENSURE THAT THE SOIL REMAINS HEALTHY

TYPES OF FLOWERS

Flowers can be classed into groups: annuals, biennials, perennials, bulbs, including the very similar rhizomes and tubers, as well as flowering shrubs and climbers. Each group has its own characteristics, and the trick is to grow flowers in the conditions that suit them. There are so many flowers to choose from that it is not worth persevering with those that are unsuitable for the conditions of your garden.

ANNUALS

Annuals grow from seed, flower, set their seeds and die, all within a year. This rapid growth makes them ideal for filling gaps in borders. Few plants give you such an abundance of blooms so quickly, and most keep flowering for months. Some of our best-loved flowers are annuals (or are best treated as such): pansies, zinnias, Iceland poppies, petunias and many more. Almost all annuals like sun and fertile soil, they like to be watered and mulched, and they can be grown from seed or seedlings.

Annuals are classed in two main groups: hardy annuals that can be sown directly in the ground in autumn or spring, and half-hardy annuals that are grown under cover and planted out when all danger of frost has passed. Fill a tray with a seed sowing mixture. There are organic composts available, or make your own with finely sieved material from the bottom of the compost heap mixed with horticultural sand. Sow the seeds thinly on the surface and, except for very fine seeds, cover with a thin layer of sowing mixture. Put a piece of glass or cling film over the tray to retain moisture and keep in a warm place or a gently heated propagator out of direct sunlight. Remove the cover when you see the first signs of germination. Transplant seedlings to individual pots as soon as they have two or three pairs of leaves.

Once the plants begin to flower, they can be given extra encouragement with a little blood and bone or liquid manure. Pick spent flowers off, to prevent the plants devoting energy to unwanted seed. This will keep them in bloom for longer. You can leave some seedheads on the plants so that you can save your own seeds for next year, but remember that most hybrid types will not breed true.

BIENNIALS

Biennials grow leaves in their first year and in their second produce flowers and seed, then they die. Foxgloves, wallflowers, forget-me-nots and stocks are biennial but all come in strains which, if they are planted early enough, will flower in their first year and so can be thought of as annuals. Parsley is the most common real biennial in gardens. Apart from their two-year lifestyle, biennials are grown in the same way as annuals, being started from seed and given good soil.

PERENNIALS

Most perennials are like biennials in that they do not always flower in their first year from seed; the difference is that they do not die after that flowering. They go on for at least another year, often for many years after that, but unlike trees and shrubs, they do not make permanent woody stems. Few flower for as long as annuals, so plan your plantings carefully for a long season of colour. This is why perennials are usually grown in mixed beds.

Perennials can be subdivided into two groups: herbaceous perennials, which have top growth that dies down for the winter each year, and evergreen perennials, like pinks, which keep at least their leaves for the winter even if the flowering stems die back.

Although perennials can be grown from seed they are more usually propagated by dividing their clumps. As they are more or less permanent denizens of the garden, it is worth preparing their positions well with compost or manure. Most can be dug up and divided every so often and the ground refreshed with more organic material, which also allows you the opportunity of transplanting the plants into new arrangements. The frequency with which you do this depends on how rapidly the variety spreads, but there is no need to do it unless the clumps are getting overcrowded and flowering is declining.

While there are many perennials that like rich soil and sun, they are less uniform in their needs than annuals, and there are perennials to suit every garden situation. Some like rich soil, others poorer soil; some like sun, and some shade; some prefer a warmer climate, others a cooler one; and so on. Most perennials appreciate being mulched.

The main problems with most perennials are snails, which adore their soft young shoots, and their often floppy stems – a display of perennials is often underpinned with a lot of stakes and string!

LEFT: *Pinks are a favourite cottage-garden perennial. Modern types flower for a long period in summer.* CENTRE: *Daffodils are among the easiest of flowers to care for; plant the bulbs in autumn and enjoy the cheerful yellow flowers in spring.* RIGHT: *Pinks again, with their distant cousin the snow-in-summer* (Cerastium tomentosum). *Both are drought-resistant.*

BULBS

Most bulbs like sun or light shade and well-drained, fertile soil. Before planting, prepare the bed well, with plenty of well-rotted manure or compost. Any kind of soil is suitable for most bulbs as long as it is well drained; bulbs will soon rot in poorly-drained soil. If the soil is heavy, dig it over deeply and put a layer of grit or sharp sand in the planting hole. The depth of planting varies with the bulb – plant at two to three times the depth of the bulb in normal soils, and at one to two times the depth in heavy soils.

After the flowers fade allow the foliage to die down naturally. Give a plentiful supply of potash at this time to encourage the development of flowers the following year. Bulbs in pots will benefit from a couple of feeds with liquid manure. Remove and compost the foliage when it has died back.

If you want to clear the beds or the bulbs are not winter-hardy, they can then be lifted, dried off and stored in a dark, well-ventilated place until planting time. Normally bulbs can be left in place to multiply, only lifting them when they get too crowded.

FLOWERING SHRUBS

These will form the backbone of a garden border. There are lots to choose from that, as well as having a decorative effect, will provide flowers, berries and shelter, attracting birds, butterflies and other insects. If planted in well-prepared ground and watered well while establishing, they should only require an annual mulch of well-rotted organic matter.

CLIMBERS

Climbing plants are invaluable in any garden, decorating arches and trellises and softening and enhancing the look of walls and fences. They need good soil preparation, especially if they are being grown against a house wall where the soil tends to be dry and poor. So dig in plenty of well-rotted organic matter before planting, give them an annual mulch, and make sure they get sufficient water.

CLOCKWISE, FROM TOP LEFT: *The Japanese iris does best in moist soil.* • *The ivy-leaved geranium is by nature a trailing plant, which makes it a favourite for container planting.* • *The dainty* Gladiolus nanus *flowers early in spring.* • *Many dahlias grow head-high and need staking, although dwarf bedding varieties such as this do not.*

A SELECTION OF FLOWERS

Here are a few suggestions for garden plants to suit a variety of habitats that will provide colour and interest over a long season and will attract lots of beneficial wildlife to your garden.

ASTER *Aster*

With their masses of daisy flowers in shades of purple, blue or pink, these plants will brighten borders at the end of the summer, as other flowers are beginning to die back, and will continue through autumn to the frosts. They provide a late supply of nectar for butterflies and other insects. The main problem is that many are prone to powdery mildew, particularly in dry, poor soils, so be sure to water them well and give them a rich soil with lots of organic matter. However, there are some outstanding varieties that are mildew-resistant, such as *Aster* x *frikartii* and varieties of *A. novae-angliae*.

AUBRIETA *Aubrieta*

This popular rock garden plant thrives in walls and dry sites and the colourful masses of flowers in various shades of purple provide nectar for early hoverflies, butterflies and other insects.

BERGAMOT *Monarda didyma*

A member of the mint family, bergamot is also known as bee balm and, as this name implies, it is a useful plant for bees and other insects. It makes a good companion for plants that need insect pollination and is a useful border plant for moist soils. There are many garden varieties of this hardy perennial, with aromatic leaves and brilliant red, purple, pink or white flowers in summer. Dig in lots of organic matter before planting, and mulch it well with leaves, straw or compost each year. Water well.

BORAGE *Borago officinalis*

Borage is a tall, fast-growing annual with bristly leaves and bright blue star-shaped flowers. Although borage can become rather straggly late in the season, in compensation it is a good mineral accumulator

Aubrieta flourishes in dry, sunny spots and the masses of colourful flowers will soften the hard lines of walls and paving and will provide valuable nectar for insects in spring.

and makes good compost material when it gets too large. It is a good companion plant, especially for strawberries. Borage does best in moist, well-mulched soils in a sunny spot. The leaves have a mild, cucumberish taste and can be added to salads and drinks such as Pimms, but be careful when handling them, as they may cause contact dermatitis. The blue flowers can be used in salads or drinks, or crystallized for cake decorations.

BUDDLEJA *Buddleja*

Known as the butterfly bush, the fragrant flowers of the buddleja not only attract butterflies but also insects of all kinds. Give this shrub a sunny site and a fertile, well-drained soil.

BUGLE *Ajuga reptans*

Bugle forms attractive mats of leaves which make good, weed-suppressing ground cover for the front of a border. It has a long flowering period and the blue spires of flowers are attractive to bees and early butterflies. Some varieties have attractive foliage in shades of bronze, purple, pink and cream.

CAMPANULA *Campanula*

The campanulas, or bellflowers, are a large family with something for every garden. There are annuals, biennials and hardy perennials; from creeping forms for the rock garden to those with tall spikes for the cottage garden border. The flowers are typically bell-shaped, in shades of blue, with some pinks and whites, and are much loved by bees.

CARNATIONS, SWEET WILLIAMS AND PINKS *Dianthus*

Carnations are short-lived perennials. Like most greyish-leaved plants they prefer sunshine and good drainage, but they do not need an especially rich soil: there is no need to lavish compost on them. They do, however, like alkaline soil, so if necessary add a little lime. Watch out for aphids, but carnation rust and collar rot should give no trouble if the site is sunny and the drainage good. Replace plants with rooted cuttings every three or four years.

The genus *Dianthus* is large, including the Sweet William, a biennial or annual (according to variety) that likes rich soil, and pinks, a large group of low-growing perennials. They like sun and a touch of lime in the soil but not too much organic matter. Almost all these dianthi have delightfully fragrant flowers and are excellent for cutting.

Chives look particularly good when used as an edging to borders and paths. Plant them round rose, fruit or vegetable beds as they make excellent companion plants.

CATMINT *Nepeta*

Well-known for being attractive to cats, catmint or catnip is a spreading perennial with aromatic grey-green leaves and lavender blue flowers. As a member of the mint family it should be kept moist at all times. Mulch lightly in spring and autumn, and feed with nitrogen-rich fertilizer such as poultry manure in spring for more leafy growth. It is a useful underplanting in rose beds, not only providing good ground cover, but also attracting beneficial insects. Not only is it an attractive plant for the flower border, it can also be planted near vegetables as it is said to deter flea beetles.

CHIVES *Allium schoenoprasum*

As well as being an essential part of any herb garden, chives can make an attractive addition to any garden border. Their pink drumstick heads of flowers are as pretty as any other border plant, and they are believed to benefit other plants growing nearby. They are recommended as companions for roses, carrots, grapes, tomatoes and fruit trees, and are also said to prevent scab on apples, blackspot on roses and aphids on many plants, especially sunflowers, chrysanthemums and tomatoes. There are other ornamental alliums which are suitable for borders and the attractive rounded heads of their flowers are much loved by beneficial insects.

CHRYSANTHEMUM
Chrysanthemum

Popular border plants for late summer and autumn, chrysanthemums come in an enormous range of colours and forms. They grow best in full sun with protection from strong winds (tall varieties will need staking) and need a rich, well-drained soil. Dig in lots of organic matter before planting and mulch regularly with compost or well-rotted manure.

If you choose to grow chrysanthemums you will need to be vigilant as they are vulnerable to several pests and diseases. Watch out for aphids, caterpillars and earwigs, which will eat the young buds. Keep these last off by smearing a touch of petroleum jelly around the stem just below the cluster of buds. A

The pretty pink flowers of Clematis montana rubens *make a marvellous display in early summer. This is the most vigorous of the clematis and is ideal for covering unsightly sheds and fences.*

number of fungal diseases can also affect them. Avoid overhead watering or watering late in the day and clear any decaying material away. If rust strikes, burn the affected plants and do not plant chrysanthemums in that bed for at least three years.

CLEMATIS *Clematis*

There are many decorative clematis to choose from, but some of the larger-flowered hybrids can be hard to establish. All clematis prefer to have their tops in the sun and a cool root run, so a thick mulch or a companion planting of evergreen ground cover will benefit them. *Clematis montana* is a vigorous grower, providing cover for nesting birds and other wildlife.

COLUMBINE *Aquilegia vulgaris*

Also known as granny's bonnets, columbines have attractive foliage and tall, spurred flowers in late spring or early summer. They do best in an open, sunny, well-drained site. The flowering season is not long, but can be prolonged by regular dead-heading. Watch out for aphids which are partial to the flowering shoots (rhubarb is said to deter them). Organic gardeners can help by preparing the bed with a bit of compost before planting. Aquilegias are not long-lived plants, but will self-sow freely.

CONEFLOWER *Echinacea*

Coneflowers are summer and autumn-flowering, providing a late season food source for insects. Their bright daisy flowers make an attractive display in the border and they are excellent for cutting. They like a fertile soil and benefit from large quantities of well-rotted manure or compost.

CONVOLVULUS
Convolvulus tricolor

The pretty trumpet flowers of this fast-growing annual supply nectar which attracts hoverflies, bees and other beneficial insects. The flowers are produced profusely from July to September.

COTONEASTER *Cotoneaster*

The cotoneasters provide a double season of interest and value, with masses of flowers in early summer, which are always buzzing with bees on a fine day, and lots of berries in the autumn, which provide food for birds. They also provide good cover for wildlife. Grow in fertile, well-drained soil.

CROCUS *Crocus*

These bulbs can be grown in borders or in grass and provide a supply of early spring pollen for beneficial insects. If you grow them in grass, do not remove the leaves too soon or the bulbs will quickly die out. If birds damage the flowers, black cotton thread tied around sticks should keep them away.

DAFFODIL *Narcissus*

Cheerful heralds of spring, daffodils are popular early flowering bulbs. There are many types to choose from, from the dainty early flowering *N. cyclamineus* to big bold hybrids suitable for bedding or naturalizing in grass or borders. Daffodil bulbs can be attacked by eelworms. The problem is uncommon, but avoid buying bulbs that are at all soft, in case they might be carrying the pest.

DAHLIA *Dahlia*

Available in a seemingly infinite variety of types, dahlias provide a bright show in the garden through summer and autumn until the first frosts. Although experts spend a lot of time pruning and thinning to produce perfect flowers, they are not difficult to grow. Plant sprouted tubers from pots in late spring in a well-prepared soil with lots of well-rotted organic matter. Choose a sunny spot, as they will not flower in shade. Water well, and pick off spent flowers to encourage a longer flowering season. Lift tubers in autumn and store in a dry, frost-free place.

DAYLILY *Hemerocallis*

Individual flowers of the daylilies only bloom for a single day, but they are produced over a long period. These are easy to grow, trouble-free plants which, depending on variety, flower from late spring to early autumn. Grow in groups for best effect, in soil enriched with organic matter. The attractive flowers come in a wide range of colours and are usually edible.

DELPHINIUM *Delphinium*

The tall blue spires of delphiniums make a striking display at the back of the border and are much loved by bees, but they are not the easiest of plants to grow. Give them a rich, well-drained soil, with plenty of well-rotted organic matter and make sure they are kept well watered. Give constant protection from slugs and snails, which love the tender young shoots, and provide support for the flower spikes.

EVENING PRIMROSE

Oenothera biennis

The evening primrose earns its name by flowering towards the end of the day. The clusters of golden-yellow flowers, borne on tall stems, are sweetly fragrant and are most strongly scented in the evening. The flowers also produce lots of pollen for insects. This is an easy to grow biennial which requires no special feeding, but it is advisable to remove the spent flowerheads as it will self-seed prolifically.

FEVERFEW

Chrysanthemum parthenium

The clusters of long-lasting white daisy-like flowers borne above low mounds of aromatic, finely cut green foliage make this an attractive plant for the front or edges of the border. The bright flowers are attractive to bees, and feverfew can be planted near fruit trees to assist pollination. The plants can be given a light mulch in spring, but do not over-feed them as this can result in too much soft, leafy growth. Do not over-water either, or the plant will rot. Otherwise, these plants have no major problems. Cut back after flowering to keep a compact shape and minimize self-seeding. There is also a golden foliaged form, and pretty double-flowered forms.

FIRETHORN *Pyracantha*

Firethorns provide spring flowers, masses of bright berries in autumn and evergreen leaves which offer cover for nesting birds and other wildlife, but site them carefully as they also have lots of sharp thorns. Pyracanthas are easy and vigorous, and can be trained against a wall or as a thorny barrier or windbreak.

FOXGLOVE *Digitalis purpurea*

Foxgloves are short-lived perennials, usually grown as annuals or biennials. They will grow in most soils in sun or shade, but do best in a cool, shady spot, with lots of organic matter in the soil. They are said to have a growth-stimulating effect on nearby plants. Their tall spires of pink, purple or white flowers will certainly brighten up the garden and they are popular with bees. Snails are their only pest. They accumulate iron, and make a useful addition to the compost heap once flowering is over. **Caution:** this plant is very poisonous (it is the source of the drug digitalis).

FRENCH MARIGOLD *Tagetes*

Not only do these half-hardy annuals provide bright, cheerful and long-lasting flowers in shades of orange, yellow and red, which will brighten any garden border or bedding scheme, they are also excellent companion plants for both the flower and vegetable garden. They attract beneficial insects such as hoverflies, and release a substance from their roots that inhibits nematodes (worms). Easy to grow, flowers should appear within a few weeks of sowing.

LEFT: *The tall spires of the foxgloves look good at the back of the border. The plants are reputed to stimulate the growth of plants around them.* CENTRE: *French marigolds are useful companion plants in both the garden and greenhouse.* RIGHT: *Fragrant climbers, such as honeysuckle, produce their flowers at a height where you can enjoy them. Grow them in a sheltered spot where the fragrance will linger.*

GERANIUM *Geranium*

The hardy geraniums are a rich and varied group of plants. They are not fussy about soil, as long as it is not waterlogged, and although most prefer sun, there are some that do better in shade, so you can find one to suit most areas of the garden. They are hardy and easy to grow, with a wide variety of leaf shapes and textures, and flowers in shades of pink, blue or purple as well as white. Many geraniums make good ground cover plants, suppressing weeds, and providing cover for overwintering creatures such as ladybirds. Although young plants may be eaten by slugs, older plants are usually trouble-free.

GLADIOLUS *Gladiolus*

The large hybrids are flowers the organic gardener should approach with caution. The problem is thrips (small insects), which destroy the flowers completely. Pyrethrum will control them, but only if sprayed every few days. The daintier early-flowering species, such as *Gladiolus carneus* and *G. byzantinus* – are fairly trouble free, and a better choice for the organic garden. Gladioli like a sunny, well-drained spot and appreciate enriched soil, so work in plenty of organic matter. Gladiolus corms (bulblike underground stems) are sometimes affected by

bacterial scab, which causes black soft patches, which eventually rot. Do not buy corms that look suspicious, and if scab does strike (it is fairly rare), get rid of any affected corms and do not grow gladioli in that bed for at least three years.

GLOBE THISTLE *Echinops ritro*

The distinctive metallic-blue flowerheads of the globe thistle make a striking display at the back of the flower border and are loved by bees. The plants need a well-drained soil, but otherwise are hardy and easy to grow. They do not require rich soil, but benefit from a feed of poultry manure in spring.

HONEYSUCKLE

Lonicera periclymenum

Honeysuckle is worth a place in the garden for its delightful fragrance alone, and it should not be hard to find a place for this climber. It is good grown against a warm wall as this will encourage the intense perfume, which will linger in sheltered spots, attracting insects, and moths on a warm night.

HYSSOP *Hyssopus officinalis*

The rich blue-violet flower spikes of hyssop are much loved by bees, which make delicious honey from them. Butterflies and other insects are also attracted to them. A decorative and easy to grow semi-evergreen shrub, hyssop has narrow, aromatic sage-green leaves. Full sun produces compact growth and more aromatic foliage, but hyssop will tolerate shade for part of the day. It will grow on reasonably fertile soil as long as it is well drained. It is said to discourage flea beetle, to lure cabbage white butterflies away from cabbages and to be a good companion for grapevines, increasing the yield.

ICE PLANT *Sedum spectabile*

Tough, reliable and easy to grow, the ice plants provide flat heads of pink autumn flowers which are loved by butterflies as well as insects of all kinds.

IRIS *Iris*

Irises fall into three groups, none of which is difficult to grow. Bulbous irises, including Dutch irises, get the usual spring bulb treatment and like a sunny spot to flower in spring. The dwarf forms provide valuable early pollen for bees.

Bearded irises, which grow from fleshy rhizomes, are happiest in full sun in well-drained soil with a touch of lime in it. Do not waste compost on them – if the soil is too humus-rich and moist you may have trouble with fungus rhizome rot, which can kill the plants. Beardless irises grow from rhizomes but like a humus rich soil, and most appreciate plenty of water while growing and flowering. They include the Siberian irises, the Pacific Coast irises, the Louisiana hybrids and the Japanese irises.

LADY'S MANTLE
Alchemilla mollis

Lady's mantle produces mounds of soft green leaves that make excellent ground cover, and frothy heads of lime-yellow flowers in summer. The rounded leaves collect dew and raindrops. This water was once reputed to have healing and magical powers but it is also a valuable source of water for the smaller forms of garden wildlife. Alchemilla will grow in any soil, in sun or partial shade, and is widely used as an edging for borders and paths.

LAVENDER *Lavandula*

One of the most popular of all the traditional cottage garden plants, lavender is an evergreen bushy shrub with aromatic, narrow, grey-green leaves and spikes of delightfully fragrant mauve flowers in summer, which are attractive to bees and butterflies. It grows best in an open sunny position in well-drained soil. Tender varieties may benefit from winter mulching.

LILY *Lilium*

There are lots of beautiful lilies for the borders, and most give good results in ordinary, well-drained garden soil, though there are some that prefer lime while others will not thrive if lime is present. Enrich the soil with well-rotted organic material before planting, and mulch annually with compost or leafmould. Snails adore the young shoots, but the big worry is aphids, which spread viral diseases, almost always fatal to lilies. If a favourite lily does succumb to a virus, you can save it by taking seeds.

LUPIN *Lupinus*

As well as being pretty and easy to grow, both annual and perennial garden lupins are good green manures because they are legumes and so can add nitrogen to the soil. They also produce root secretions that can

The pretty, fragrant spikes of lavender are alive with bees, butterflies and all manner of insects on warm summer days. Lavender is a popular choice of plant for any garden.

make phosphates more available in the soil. Lupins are noted for their ability to suppress weeds, and are also said to be good companions for roses.

They can be grown as 'trap' plants, attracting aphids after flowering, and the ladybirds and other predators that feed on them.

■■ NASTURTIUM *Tropaeolum majus*

As well as producing decorative flowers in shades of orange and other warm colours, all parts of the nasturtium are edible. Both leaves and flowers are tasty and nutritious, and the flowers make a colourful addition to salads. The seeds and unopened flower buds can be pickled as a substitute for capers. Not only are they pretty and useful, these annuals are very easy to grow. Do not plant them in rich soil or over-water them, however, or you will get lots of lush leaves at the expense of flowers. Although they grow in shady positions, they flower best in a sunny spot. Aphids love nasturtiums, but this does mean that they make excellent companion plants for vegetables such as cabbages, broccoli and other brassicas, the idea being that the aphids will flock to them and leave the vegetables alone. Grow nasturtiums around apple trees to reduce problems with woolly aphids. If you do not want to use them as companion plants and aphids are a problem on the plants, pinch off small numbers or try vigorously hosing the pest off if it is present in larger numbers.

■■ PEONY *Paeonia*

Peonies are popular for their handsome flowers and attractive foliage, but can be difficult to establish and dislike root disturbance. Plant in good rich soil, preferably with a touch of lime in it, in a position where they will not be disturbed. They like an annual mulch of old manure in early spring. Keep a watch out for pests as caterpillars like the young shoots and earwigs like the developing buds.

■■ POACHED EGG PLANT
Limnanthes douglasii

The bright yellow and white flowers give this plant its common name of poached egg plant. The plants

The poached egg plant is useful as a companion plant in all areas of the garden because it is very attractive to hoverflies, bees and other beneficial insects.

are low-growing and can be grown at the front of borders and as fillers in the flower or vegetable garden. They can also be used for inter-cropping or planted under taller growing plants as a weed-suppressing green manure. Try them under soft fruit, roses and shrubs.

■■ POT MARIGOLD
Calendula officinalis

The pot marigold is an easy to grow annual for the border or herb garden, attracting hoverflies and other beneficial insects. The petals of its orange daisy flowers are edible and make a colourful addition to salads and drinks. Another traditional cottage garden favourite, it blooms from May to the first frosts, and readily self-seeds from one year to the next. Dead-heading will prolong flowering.

■■ PRIMROSE *Primula vulgaris*

The primrose is a much-loved flower and we welcome its delicate yellow flowers as harbingers of spring. Well-suited to a woodland or shady garden, it can start flowering very early in sheltered places and provides nectar for several early butterflies.

ROSES

Few gardeners can resist roses but the average how-to-grow-roses book is a bit off-putting for organic gardeners. You are advised to give bushes regular doses of artificial fertilizers and spray them with chemicals from one end of the growing season to the other. The best alternative is to grow only varieties with a proven record of health in your area.

Give roses an open, sunny position. They are not too fussy about soil as long as they do not have to put up with wet feet. Very sandy soil is not to their liking, but even there the noble *Rosa rugosa* and its varieties will flourish. (These are the toughest and most disease- and pest-proof of all roses.) Roses love the richest possible soil, but are no more dependent on artificial fertilizer than any other plant. Prepare the soil well, turning in plenty of well-rotted manure and compost. Mulch the bushes each year after winter pruning. Water at the root: wet foliage encourages black spot.

Fungus diseases, particularly mildew, black spot and rust, are the main problems. Mildew is a nuisance, and is worst when the plant roots are dry. If you see it, give the bushes a thorough watering. Dark red roses are apt to be more susceptible;

varieties with glossy foliage are usually resistant. Many of the 'Old Roses' will mildew, but only when the flowers are over. While it looks awful, it does not affect their growth very much.

Black spot penetrates the leaf, and by the time you see the distinctive fringed black spots, it is too late. If black spot is not treated, the infected leaf will infect others and die. A bad attack can strip the plant. Spores only grow on a leaf that has been wet for a few hours, so avoid watering the foliage. Good hygiene, removing and burning infected leaves as soon as you see them, is a help, but growing resistant varieties is the best preventative. Yellow, orange and flame varieties are apt to be prone to black spot, whereas *R. bracteata* is said to be immune. Growing garlic or onions with roses is said to help prevent black spot. As a last resort, approved sprays, such as dispersible sulphur, can be used. Spray at dusk to reduce risk to beneficial insects.

Rust is even more devastating. Again, the best approach is to grow the least susceptible varieties, and to remove and burn any infected leaves straight away. If you really need to spray, Bordeaux mixture (see p. 85) is the most effective treatment.

Recommended companion plants include garlic, chives, parsley, mignonette, lupins and catmint.

ABOVE: Rosa rugosa *is amongst the toughest and most pest- and disease-resistant of the roses.* LEFT: *Catmint is a useful underplanting, providing good ground cover and attracting beneficial insects.*

RED HOT POKER *Kniphofia*

Striking border plants with bright flower spikes and grassy evergreen foliage, red hot pokers are tough, easy to grow, hardy perennials that will tolerate a wide range of conditions, including exposed, windy or coastal areas. Give them a sunny position and well-drained soil. Although they tolerate poor soils, they will give a better show in soils enriched with well-rotted manure or compost. Bees are frequent visitors, clambering inside the tubular flowers to reach the rich supply of nectar, and the grassy crowns provide a winter home for insects.

ROCK ROSE *Cistus*

Rock roses are outstandingly drought-resistant. Give them sun, sharp drainage and a sheltered spot and they will produce compact healthy bushes with a long succession of pretty summer flowers in a range of old-rose colours. Like many aromatic-leaved plants they are seldom troubled by pests and diseases.

SNOWDROP *Galanthus*

Snowdrops are always a welcome sight in late winter and early spring, and are also a welcome source of pollen for early insects.

SUNFLOWER *Helianthus*

Big, bold and cheery, the sunny yellow heads of the sunflowers will brighten any garden and these are very useful plants in many ways. The flowers are attractive to beneficial insects, including bees, butterflies, lacewings and predatory wasps, and the seeds provide food for the birds. Tall-growing, they can be grown as a decorative screen, and will produce a lot of bulky leaf and stem material which can be added to the compost heap.

SWEET PEA *Lathyrus odoratus*

Sweet peas love a rich, deeply cultivated soil, and a boost with manure water when the flowering season is well advanced will prolong the display. Like most annuals they flower for longer if they are not allowed to set seed. Being legumes, the spent plants are very desirable additions to the compost heap.

TULIP *Tulipa*

Tulips are much admired spring flowers, adding splashes of strong colour to spring borders, and are easy to grow. Give them a well-drained position, sheltered from strong winds. Keep a watch out for aphids, which may infest young growth if not dealt with quickly. Bulbs may be eaten by slugs or mice.

VIOLETS *Viola*

The sweet violet *(Viola odorata)* is a traditional and much loved early spring flower, popular for its delicate, sweetly scented blooms. These are usually violet in colour, but can be mauve, blue or white. Low-growing perennials, they make good ground cover in partly shaded areas, but don't grow them in too much shade or they may be shy flowering. They tolerate most soils, but do best in deep soil, rich in well-rotted organic matter, preferably from composted fallen leaves. The flowers are edible.

Garden violets and pansies *(Viola* x *wittrockiana)* are popular for bedding and do well in mixed cottage-style borders where they benefit from the shade of other plants. Dead-head to prolong flowering.

WALLFLOWER *Cheiranthus*

Always popular for their delightful fragrance and colourful flowers early in the year, they are closely related to cabbages, and like them can be affected by club root so grow them in a different place each year.

YARROW *Achillea*

The native yarrow *(Achillea millefolium)* produces flat, white flowerheads over a long season, which are very attractive to beneficial insects. Yarrow is well known as a companion plant, and has been called the 'herb doctor'. It is reputed to increase the health and disease resistance of other plants and to increase the aromatic quality of herbs. It is also used as a compost activator in biodynamic gardening. The native yarrow is often considered a weed but some attractive and colourful forms have been bred for the garden border, such as *A.m.* 'Cerise Queen', *A.* 'Coronation Gold', 'Moonshine', 'Fanal' and many more, which are still attractive to insects.

HEALTHY ORGANIC
VEGETABLES

WHEN YOU GROW VEGETABLES ORGANICALLY YOU CAN BE
SURE YOU ARE NOT EATING CHEMICAL RESIDUES

In many cases gardeners become interested in organic gardening because they do not want to eat chemicals with their food. By growing your own you can be sure, too, that your vegetables will be absolutely fresh, with all the advantages in flavour and nourishment that this gives. You can choose the very best cultivars, which are not always the ones favoured by the market gardener, who has to consider such things as the size of the crop and how well it will stand up to rough handling in the market – no one will buy a bruised tomato, no matter how delicious it might be.

Even so, there is little point in growing your own unless you can match the market gardeners for quality. Undersized vegetables are no reward for your time and effort. Happily, growing top-quality vegetables is not at all difficult, and it can be done without recourse to chemical fertilizers and toxic sprays. The secret is simple – grow them as quickly as possible. Allow growth to slow down, and you will have woody carrots, tough cabbages and under-sized lettuces which will probably bolt into flower prematurely. And a plant that is growing well is more able to shake off pests and diseases.

LAYING OUT THE GARDEN

Give your vegetable patch the best location you can, with as much sunshine as possible, shelter from the wind and protection from romping dogs and playing children. How big it should be depends on your ambitions and the size of the family. As a very rough guide, about 35–40m^2 (38–44yd^2) should provide enough for a family of four. Tradition places the vegetable garden in an inconspicuous position in the back garden, but there is no reason why you should hide it away. If you like, you can include some flowers among the vegetables, as companion plants, for cutting or simply for decoration.

The time-honoured method of growing most vegetables is in straight rows, which makes them easier to care for. Allow access space every few rows for tending the plants and harvesting. An alternative is to use a system of deep beds, as described on page 63. Plan on growing a variety rather than a large amount of just a few types of vegetable, even if they are your favourites. Nothing is more certain to make your family discover a sudden loathing for peas or pumpkins than their appearance at every meal.

CROP ROTATION

However you lay out your vegetable beds, you should make a plan – maybe numbering the beds – to show what you are planting where. Should you have too many cabbages, say, or not enough, it will remind you to adjust your quantities next time. More importantly, it makes rotating crops easier to organize, for without a plan it is surprisingly easy to forget just which bed was given to cabbages when.

Crop rotation is simple in principle: do not plant the same crop in the same bed two years running. The reason for this is twofold. First, it avoids the chance of any crop's particular pests and diseases building up. Second, by grouping vegetables according to their soil and nutrient requirements, it helps get the best value from your crops and your compost. The need to grow vegetables quickly means they must have rich soil, and that means the vegetable garden will take most of your compost. However, not all need their soil equally enriched, and not all enjoy the same growing conditions. For example, peas and brassicas like well-limed soil but potatoes do not. Another factor to consider in grouping crops is the sowing and harvesting times.

Some fast-growing vegetables, such as lettuce, are valuable for inter-cropping or as catch crops, making the most of ground between the main crop rotations. Others benefit from a small permanent bed of their own, outside the main crop rotation system. These tend to be crops such as asparagus that are perennials and can be grown in the same beds for many years.

The simplest technique is to divide the vegetable garden into three or four beds and follow a rotation. For example, dig in lots of well-rotted manure for potatoes, sweet corn and the squash family in the first year as these are greedy feeders. Lime the ground for a crop of peas and beans the following year. Make a compost trench over winter for runner beans. In the third year, grow the cabbage family, which will benefit from the lime applied the previous year as well as from the nitrogen from the legumes. In the fourth year grow root crops. Not heavy feeders, they should not be given fresh manure, but well-rotted compost can be dug in in the previous autumn. Use green manure crops each winter on bare plots.

However, do not feel you have to keep rigidly to this system; adapt it to suit your needs. You may have vegetables that you choose not to grow, or you may prefer to concentrate on salads or exotic crops.

A well-kept vegetable garden can be extremely satisfying to the eye, simply from the ordered marshalling of crops in various shades of green in their straight lines.

Deep beds can be used to make optimum use of the space in a vegetable garden and will produce much higher yields than a conventional plot.

LEFT: *Plant sweet corn in blocks, so that the pollen falling from the tassels will alight on the silks and fertilize the female flowers.* CENTRE: *The tomato is one of those obliging plants that continues to flower even as the first fruits begin to ripen. Let the fruit ripen as red as this on the vine.* RIGHT: *Courgettes can be picked at any time once the flowers wither. The flower itself is edible.*

Getting started

First make sure the soil has been well dug, weeded and suitably enriched, then decide whether to use seed or seedlings. It is unlikely that seedlings you buy will have been grown without artificial fertilizer or fungicides and that may be a concern, although any residues should have vanished by the time the plants come to harvest. Most seeds from major suppliers are not grown organically, but there are now several firms that supply a good range of organic vegetable seeds by mail order. You can also save your own seed for next year from your choicest plants. This is easy to do: gather the seeds when they are ripe, dry them off in a cool place out of the sun and store them, absolutely dry, in airtight containers, preferably in the vegetable compartment of the fridge.

It is useless, however, to save the seed of F1 or F2 hybrid varieties. They can only be perpetuated by breeding the hybrid afresh each time seed is wanted. Some organic gardeners disapprove of them but they do often possess superior vigour, health, and sometimes flavour, to 'open-pollinated' varieties; so most gardeners feel there is no reason not to grow them unless they plan to save their own seed.

Pests and diseases

The succulence that makes vegetables good eating for us makes them attractive to pests, and while the odd bug hole in a cabbage leaf does not matter, you do not want pests consuming the best part of the harvest. Here prevention is better than cure. Good soil management and the correct growing conditions should keep your plants in a healthy condition and better able to withstand problems. Rotating crops so that pests do not build up in any particular bed is essential and companion planting can help too, as does regular checking of crops so that you can deal with any problems before they become too extensive.

Fortunately, there is no need for toxic sprays. Choose resistant varieties, where available. Some pests, such as slugs and snails, can be trapped, while physical barriers will keep off others, such as carrot fly. There are also an increasing number of biological controls available. Aphids and insects such as bean fly and onion fly will almost always succumb to pyrethrum (see page 85). Use sprays as a last resort, and you should be scrupulous about observing the manufacturer's withholding time, that is, the period after spraying before the vegetable will be safe to eat.

SOLANACEAE

POTATO *Solanum tuberosum*

The potato will grow even on poor land and is the best of all 'cleaning crops' – if you are faced with new or neglected, weedy ground, plant a crop of potatoes on it and they will crowd out the weeds – and digging up the crop will be splendid cultivation for whatever you want to plant next.

Growing and Harvesting

Although the soil need not be rich, potatoes will give you a better crop in well-drained fertile soils with lots of organic matter dug in. Avoid limy soil as this will increase the chances of scab disease. Always buy seed potatoes that have been certified disease-free. Choose a mix of early, second early and main crop varieties for a long cropping season. Chit (sprout) the potatoes by placing them in shallow trays in a cool, light position. Plant out in early to mid-spring. Set the tubers 30–40cm (12–20in) apart in rows spaced twice that, and put them 15cm (6in) deep. Earlier crops can be obtained by planting 'earlies' under cloches or black polythene in late winter.

When the shoots come up, mound soil over them if frost is still a threat. When the stems are about 23cm (9in) high, earth up the rows, or add a thick, rough mulch. This will exclude sunlight from the developing tubers and protect them from blight.

Potato flowers are not anything to write home about, but when they appear you can start scrabbling around for your first tiny new potatoes – one of the delights of vegetable growing. They will not keep, so take them the day you are going to eat them. And do not take too many, or the main crop will suffer.

About three weeks after flowering is finished, the lowest leaves turn yellow and you can then dig up a few plants for early potatoes. They will not store for long, so only dig them as you want them. Dig main-crop potatoes in autumn, as the foliage begins to die back. Cut the stems to ground level then leave for one to two weeks before forking out the tubers. Leave to dry for a few hours before storing. Store only the perfect tubers; use any blemished ones immediately.

Problems

Aphids will probably appear with the young leaves and you should deal with them in the usual way as they spread viral diseases. Blight can strike in warm, humid weather. It starts out as yellow spots and patches on the leaves, which rot. If left uncontrolled, it will rot the tubers, too. Cut off and burn contaminated foliage as soon as any symptoms are seen and treat with a copper-based spray such as Bordeaux mixture (see page 85) in mid-summer, and from then on at fortnightly intervals until harvesting. Scab can be avoided by growing resistant varieties in soils with plenty of organic matter and watering well during dry spells.

Companions

Potatoes do well with peas, beans, sweet corn, cabbage, nasturtiums and marigolds. Horseradish is said to help by destroying eelworms.

TOMATO *Lycopersicon esculentum*

Few gardeners can resist growing a few tomato plants, either under cover in the greenhouse or outdoors in garden beds. Some of the newer varieties, such as 'Tumbler', will even grow well in containers. All tomato plants like a sunny position and rich soil as well as plenty of water while the plants are growing, although the flavour is said to be even better if you ease off on the watering once the first fruits begin to ripen.

Growing and Harvesting

Sow seed under glass in early spring and prick out seedlings into individual pots to grow on. Harden off outdoor varieties and plant out once all danger of frost has passed. Tie upright varieties to canes and remove side shoots as they grow. Pinch out the tops when the plants have made four to six trusses. Bush varieties do not need staking or pinching out, but, as they tend to sprawl, spread straw underneath them to help keep the fruit clean.

Keep the plants well-watered and feed with a liquid manure at approximately fortnightly intervals once the fruit begins to develop.

Pick as soon as the fruits are ripe. Help end-of-season green fruits to ripen by laying them on straw and covering with cloches.

PROBLEMS

Greenhouse tomatoes are subject to a range of problems. Deal with aphids in the usual way. Tackle whitefly by hanging sticky cards above the crop, or by introducing the parasitic wasp *Encarsia formosa*. Discourage red spider mites by keeping humidity high or by introducing the predatory mite *Phytoseiulus persimilis.* A derris spray can be used, but not if biological controls have already been introduced. Nematodes (worms) can affect tomato roots; asparagus and marigolds are said to discourage them. Tomatoes can also be subject to potato blight.

COMPANIONS

French marigolds are good companions, encouraging growth, deterring nematodes and attracting pollinating insects. Others include asparagus, basil, nasturtiums, stinging nettles and, some say, parsley.

▦ PEPPERS *Capsicum annuum*

Capsicums and chillis, known as sweet peppers and hot peppers respectively, are tropical plants, liking heat and moisture. They can be grown outdoors, generally under cloches, in warm, sheltered areas, but will do best in a greenhouse.

GROWING AND HARVESTING

Sow in warmth in early spring and prick out the sturdiest seedlings into individual pots for growing on. If growing outside, harden off before planting out after danger of frost has passed. Tie the plants to canes as they grow, water regularly and, once the fruit has set, feed with a liquid manure every one to two weeks. Mist flowers of greenhouse plants to help fruit to set and to discourage red spider mite.

You can pick fruit as soon as they are big enough to be useful. Chillis are hotter if left to ripen fully.

PROBLEMS

As for tomatoes (see page 25).

COMPANIONS

Capsicums grow well with basil.

▦ AUBERGINE *Solanum melongena*

Aubergines, or eggplants, are more successful in the greenhouse than out of doors, but can succeed under cloches in warm, sunny gardens.

GROWING AND HARVESTING

Grow as for peppers. For the best crop of fruit, pinch out growing tips and further flowers once five or six fruit have formed, and feed with liquid manure at weekly intervals. Do not over-water as the plants are susceptible to root rot. Mulch around the plants to help maintain even moisture and temperature levels in the soil.

Cut (do not pick) the fruit when it has developed its full colour, but do not let it get so ripe that the skin begins to wrinkle or it will be tough.

PROBLEMS

Aphids, whitefly and red spider mites are main pests.

COMPANIONS

Basil is the traditional companion plant.

CUCURBITACEAE

▦ CUCUMBER *Cucumis sativus*

There are many forms: for outdoor or greenhouse growth; bush or trailing varieties; long, short or round fruit, but they are all greedy crops – it is hard to give them too much compost or old manure. All-female greenhouse varieties are prolific and easy to grow, but do not grow them with standard varieties, as any male flowers will pollinate the all-female types and result in bitter, distorted fruits.

GROWING AND HARVESTING

Sow under cover in spring, two to a pot, and thin to the strongest seedling. The plants are short-growing vines. You can allow them to sprawl on the ground, but it is better to train them on trellis or canes and wires as the fruit does not get muddy and the leaves

are less likely to get mildewed. Tie in regularly and trim the side shoots to encourage bushy growth. Feed with liquid manure at one- to two-week intervals. Cucumbers have a high water requirement and should be kept moist at all times. They also like a humid atmosphere, so spray greenhouse plants, staging and paths daily. Pick young fruit regularly to encourage the development of more fruit.

PROBLEMS

Slugs, aphids and red spider mites can be a problem. Cucumber mosaic virus is carried by aphids, so deal with aphids rapidly if seen. The virus causes leaves to become mottled and yellow and stunts growth. Affected plants should be destroyed. Powdery mildew can also be a problem. Remove and burn affected leaves and, if necessary, spray with a copper-based fungicide.

COMPANIONS

Chives are said to keep mildew away. Nasturtiums are also traditional companions, used to lure away whitefly. Cucumbers grow well with peas, beans, lettuce, radishes, sweet corn and sunflowers.

FROM TOP: *To avoid cutting them in half, always dig potatoes with a fork. • White or mauve potato flowers are the sign that the first new potatoes are ready. • Red radishes are the kind used for salads and are most tender when small. • The mild-flavoured giant white radish or daikon is a favourite vegetable in Chinese and Japanese cooking.*

▨ COURGETTES AND MARROWS *Cucurbita*

Courgettes are really marrows, picked when young, and both are grown in the same way.

GROWING AND HARVESTING

They are greedy feeders, so prepare the ground with plenty of well-rotted organic material. They can be grown in full sun or partial shade, but prefer a sheltered site. Sow under cover in spring, or outdoors in late spring. Sow two seeds to a station and thin to the strongest. Keep weed-free, but do not cultivate too deeply or you risk damaging the shallow roots. A mulch of well-rotted material will help keep weeds down and moisture in, but do not use fresh manure or over-feed as this will promote leaves at the expense of fruit. Pick the fruit as small as you please – more will follow. If allowed to mature, they become marrows.

PROBLEMS

Aphids, powdery mildew and bacterial wilt can be a problem and preventive care is important.

COMPANIONS

As for cucumbers (see page 27).

▬▬▬ PUMPKINS AND SQUASHES

Cucurbita

The classic giant pumpkins grow on enormous, sprawling vines, and the best place for them is where they can clamber over and camouflage the compost heap or the rubbish pile. The smaller, bush varieties are more suited to the average garden.

GROWING AND HARVESTING

Squashes have a long growing period and need a good soil, so dig in plenty of well-rotted organic material. Sow under cover in spring, planting out when all danger of frost has passed. Allow plenty of room, spacing at least 90cm (3ft) apart. Nip out the growing tips to encourage fruiting laterals and feed with liquid manure at fortnightly intervals from midsummer. You can pick the fruit as soon as it is ripe, but flavour is best, and they keep better, if you wait until the vine dies off in autumn.

PROBLEMS/COMPANIONS

As for other cucurbits.

LEGUMINOSAE

Legumes can fix their own nitrogen from the air, so they do not need very rich soil; a spot that was previously manured for a leaf crop will suit them very well. Add lime if the soil is on the acid side. After cropping add the plants to the compost heap.

▬▬▬ BROAD BEANS   *Vicia fabia*

As well as producing a good, nutritious early crop of beans, these are excellent green manure crops.

GROWING AND HARVESTING

Sow in autumn, under cloches, from early spring to

LEFT: *Capsicums have bell-shaped fruit that hang down.* CENTRE: *Most (though not all) chillis point upwards. They get hotter as they ripen; for maximum hotness, do not water once they begin to do so.* RIGHT: *Eggplants make a coarse-leaved, top-heavy bush. The horizontal wire you can just see is strung between two stakes to support a row of plants.*

early summer, in double drills about 5cm (2in) deep and 10cm (4in) apart. Support the growing plants, especially in exposed areas, with string tied to posts. Mulch between rows and make sure they have sufficient water, but do not over-water as wet soil can lead to root diseases.

Pick regularly when young and tender to encourage further pods, or for a main crop of beans gather pods when seeds are large but not bulging.

PROBLEMS

Pinch out growing tips above the flowers to discourage blackfly or spray with insecticidal soap. Reduce likelihood of problems with chocolate spot by good cultivation and adequate feeding. Remove and burn affected plants at the first sign of problems, and spray the others with a copper fungicide. Pea and bean weevils can be treated with derris if necessary.

COMPANIONS

A row of tansy, spinach or summer savory next to the beans is said to repel blackfly, and savory is a great seasoning for beans in the kitchen, too. Beans also grow well with carrots, cauliflower and beets.

FRENCH OR STRING BEAN
Phaseolus vulgaris

This is one of those vegetables that is always nicest picked young and tender from your own garden. Varieties come with strings or without and are classed either as 'climbing' or 'bush'. The bushes do not need support and they mature earlier, but the climbers crop more heavily and for longer. They can be given old-fashioned beanpoles for support, or you could do as the American Indians used to and sow beans at the foot of sweet corn plants when these are about 30cm (12in) tall, making sure that you water sufficiently for both.

GROWING AND HARVESTING

Make early spring sowings under cloches and follow with successional unprotected sowings for a long cropping season. Set seeds about 5cm (2in) deep and

15cm (6in) apart. Keep weed-free and mulch between plants with compost. Pick the young beans regularly, before the seeds swell, to prolong the crop.

PROBLEMS
Generally trouble-free, but keep a watch for aphids.

COMPANIONS
As for other beans.

RUNNER BEAN
Phaseolus coccineus
Popular and heavy cropping, these climbers also have attractive flowers and can make quite a decorative display in the vegetable garden.

GROWING AND HARVESTING
They need fertile, moisture-retentive ground for a good crop and should be kept well mulched and watered throughout the growing season. Sow in heat in April for hardening off and planting out in late May, or sow direct outdoors once danger of frost has passed. Provide sturdy canes for support.

Pick regularly when young and tender; this will encourage further production.

PROBLEMS
Slugs, aphids and red spider mite can be problems.

COMPANIONS
As for other beans. Increase yields by growing with flowers that attract pollinating insects.

PEA *Pisum sativum*
New peas fresh from the garden are one of the great joys of growing your own vegetables.

GROWING AND HARVESTING
Grow a succession of early and main crops for a long picking season. The earliest crops can be sown in the autumn under cloches and overwintered as long as the winter is not too hard. Later crops can be sown from early spring (under cloches) to early summer. Scatter the seeds in a wide trench about 5cm (2in)

deep. Support shorter varieties with pea sticks, and taller varieties with netting. Hoe to remove weeds and mulch with well-rotted compost. Start picking peas 12–14 weeks after sowing. Pick peas young and constantly to keep the plants cropping.

PROBLEMS

Pea moth can be a serious problem. Reduce the likelihood of problems by sowing either early or late so that the peas are not in flower when the pea moth is laying its eggs in early to mid-summer. Alternatively, cover flowering plants with a fine mesh to keep the moths out. If the attack is severe, spray with derris. Pea and bean weevils can also be a problem. Birds may pull up the baby seedlings in the hope of finding peas still attached. String some black thread above the rows to deter them.

COMPANIONS

Carrots, radishes, cucumbers, sweet corn and beans.

VARIETIES

Mangetout and sugar snap peas, which you eat pod and all, are grown in the same way.

CRUCIFERAE/BRASSICAS

Brassica oleracea is one of the most versatile of plants. After centuries of cultivation, many varieties have been bred but all are grown in a similar way.

GROWING AND HARVESTING

Brassicas will be sweeter and more tender if grown fast. Start with soil enriched with plenty of compost or well-rotted manure, and add a light dressing of lime if the soil is acid. Most brassicas will benefit from a handful of compost and seaweed meal in the hole when planting out. During the growing season keep the plants well mulched and watered.

For harvesting see entries for individual crops.

PROBLEMS

Brassicas should be grown together in the rotation, and should not be grown in the same ground in consecutive years. They are all prone to the bacterial disease club root, which stunts their growth very badly. It has no cure and careful crop rotation is the only preventative, fortunately an effective one. (If you mix flowers in with your vegetables, count stocks, wallflowers and honesty as brassicas when rotating. They are related plants and also prone to club root.)

Cabbage root fly is a serious pest of the brassica family, leading to wilting, then complete collapse of the plants. To prevent the problem, make a collar of carpet underlay, roofing felt or even cardboard, about 15cm (6in) square, to put around the stems. This will prevent the adult fly laying its eggs in the soil by the stem. Otherwise, the main pests are snails and the fat green caterpillar of the cabbage white butterfly, which is easily eliminated with *Bacillus thuringiensis*.

COMPANIONS

Hyssop grown nearby is said to discourage cabbage white butterflies and even club root. Other good companions are celery, chamomile, dill, sage, peppermint, rosemary, thyme and wormwood.

▬▬ CABBAGE

Brassica oleracea var. *capitata*

Cabbage is the most versatile of the green leafy vegetables, featuring in most national cuisines. There are varieties suitable for spring, summer or winter harvest. You can plant cabbages at almost any time from early spring until autumn, making successive plantings for a year-round supply. Spacing depends on whether you want small, family-size heads or colossal ones.

The first crops of spring cabbage can be treated as leafy 'spring greens', taking out alternate plants and leaving the others to grow hearts. Otherwise, harvest cabbages when the heart feels firm. Cut them with a sharp knife; if you then cut a cross in the top of the stem new leaves will grow. A second heart is unlikely, but the tender new leaves are delicious.

As well as the ordinary cabbages, there are the delicious red cabbages and the wrinkle-leaved Savoy cabbage, grown in just the same way.

BRUSSELS SPROUTS

Brassica oleracea var. *gemmifera*

Instead of making a single heart like a cabbage, each plant produces mini-cabbages up the stalk. Sprouts are hardy, but do best in beds with firm soil and a sunny aspect. Most soil types are suitable, with the exception of sandy soils, which result in loose leafy buttons with no hearts, and waterlogged soils. Give them shelter from wind, as they are liable to get top heavy and blow over. A short stake can help, as can mounding soil around the plants. They need a longer growing period than most brassicas, taking from about 28–36 weeks, depending on variety.

They need to be started in early or mid-spring, but to make the most of the ground, fast-maturing crops can be planted between the rows during the early stages of growth. Harvest from early autumn to spring – they are said to taste best after the first frost. Cut the sprouts rather than pull them off and the plant will make a tuft of little leaves at each place. These are worth gathering – they have a different flavour but are still delicious. Remove yellowing leaves to encourage air flow around the plants and to reduce the risk of fungal infection.

Most varieties are F1 hybrids, bred to have all the sprouts ready at the same time. Non-hybrids have the advantage of maturing in succession from the bottom up, so you are less likely to have a glut. On the other hand, sprouts freeze very well.

The colour of turnips depends on the variety: some have purple tops like this one, others are completely white.

CAULIFLOWER

Brassica oleracea var. *botrytis*

Cauliflowers are perhaps the most difficult of the brassicas to grow well. They need a rich soil, are particularly susceptible to nutrient deficiencies and the delicate curds are easily damaged. Make sure the beds have plenty of well-rotted organic matter dug in and that they are well-limed. A dressing of seaweed meal should provide the trace elements they need. Mulch well and keep the soil around the plants moist for good head development, but do not water directly over the heads as this may damage them. The heads need to be protected both from direct overhead sun and from frost – as they grow, bend the top leaves over the heads to protect them.

Cut the heads while they are firm and before they become discoloured. The young leaves can also be harvested and used as greens for cooking.

The several varieties of ordinary white cauliflower really vary only in their maturing times, which range from 18–24 weeks for summer and autumn varieties and 40–50 weeks for winter kinds.

BROCCOLI

Brassica oleracea var. *italica*

Grown as annuals, there are purple-sprouting, white sprouting and green sprouting (calabrese) forms. Broccoli does best sown *in situ* in spring, but can be started in seedbeds or small pots. Feeding with liquid seaweed manure or blood, fish and bone can improve crops. Spears – young flower shoots – are harvested from mid-winter to later spring. Pick when young and tender to encourage rapid succession. Calabrese matures in summer, and after the central head is cut will produce a succession of side shoots.

KALE   *Brassica oleracea*

An exceptionally hardy brassica, kale is grown for its nutritious leafy shoots, and is harvested from November to April. There are curly and smooth leaved types. Kale is more tolerant of hard weather and poorer soils than other brassicas, but it will crop better in an open, sunny position, sheltered from cold winds, with lots of organic matter dug into the soil.

CLOCKWISE, FROM TOP LEFT:
A fine stand of European cabbages, their edibility hardly compromised by the odd bug hole. • Chinese cabbage, the type known as pei ts'ai in Mandarin, wom bok in Cantonese and sometimes as celery cabbage. • Celery, ready for harvest, either by blanching or by taking green stalks as you need them. • These kohlrabi are ready for harvest: let them get much bigger and they will be tough.

▰▰ CHINESE CABBAGE
Brassica rapa var. *pekinensis*
Several species are called Chinese cabbage but are also known by their Chinese or Japanese names, such as bok choy, wom bok and mizumi. Quick-maturing, they produce large heads in 10–12 weeks from sowing. Make successional sowings from spring to late summer and keep well mulched and watered to prevent bolting. Flea beetles, slugs and aphids will attack these plants, and they can be used as 'trap' plants to attract pests away from other crops.

▰▰ KOHLRABI
Brassica oleracea gongylodes
Although this is a member of the cabbage family, it is grown not for its leafy heads but for its swollen turnip-shaped stem, which is highly nutritious. It is an easy-to-grow, disease-resistant crop, which tolerates relatively poor conditions, and makes an excellent turnip substitute for light, sandy soils. Make successional sowings from spring to summer and start to pull them up when they are little bigger than golf balls. Do not throw the leaves away – they will still be tender enough to cook like cabbage.

▰▰ TURNIP   *Brassica rapa*
Although grown as a root vegetable, this too is a member of the brassica family, and is best grown in the same crop rotation. Make small sowings from

late winter to summer for a succession of crops from spring to autumn. Grow them in well-manured soil, kept well mulched and watered to ensure rapid growth and to prevent the roots becoming tough. They can be harvested when young, about golf-ball size, for using raw in salads, or grown on to about cricket-ball size for cooking. Turnips can be affected by flea beetle and soft rot. Soft rot is worse in wet conditions, so grow plants in well-drained soil.

Swedes (*Brassica rapa* var. *napobrassica*), also known as rutabaga, are similar to turnips, though perhaps a little sweeter and better keeping. Grow them in the same way as turnips.

▓▓ RADISH *Raphanus sativus*

Quick-growing and tolerant of a wide range of growing conditions, radishes can be grown as catch crops between rows of slower-maturing vegetables.

Although they are members of the brassica family, it is not essential to keep them in the brassica rotation, as they can be grown and harvested so fast that they do not have time to develop diseases.

Sow the seeds thinly in rows in spring, water the plants to keep them growing quickly, and in three to six weeks or so you can pull radishes for salads. Aim to finish the crop in another four weeks or so; after that the roots get too big and woody. If you fancy, you can make further sowings every three weeks or so all through summer. The soil need not be rich, as long as it is well cultivated and friable.

The main problem is flea beetle. Chervil is the traditional companion plant, and is said to make the radishes taste hotter. Radishes are also said to do well near peas, lettuce and nasturtiums. Do not grow them with hyssop (to discourage flea beetle) as these two plants do not grow well together.

Winter radishes are hardier, produce much larger roots and take two to three months to mature. Sow in summer for harvest from autumn onwards. They have a stronger flavour than summer varieties.

CLOCKWISE, FROM TOP LEFT: *Onions, ready for harvest, but they will not keep unless you wait for the foliage to wither. The plant at the back is kale, a pretty but coarse-flavoured type of cabbage. • Young carrots are caged by twigs to protect them from birds. • Ready for harvest, these carrots can still wait a while longer. • Wait until these parsnips die down before harvesting them.*

UMBELLIFERAE

▦ CARROT *Daucus carota*

Carrots are a bit fussy about their beds – they need a light, deep, stone-free soil if they are not to grow forked and misshapen. However, you can get over problem soil by growing the round or stump-rooted varieties. A heavy soil can be improved by growing a green manure crop of flax to make it more friable.

GROWING AND HARVESTING

Carrots like a position in full sun but will tolerate partial shade, and do best on light soil with plenty of well-rotted organic matter. A bed that has been heavily manured the previous season is ideal. Fresh manure will cause forked roots and poor flavour.

For a succession of crops sow at intervals from early spring to mid-summer. Make the earliest sowings under cloches to get them off to a good start. Sow in shallow drills and thin to about 8cm (3in) apart. Carrots can be pulled young, before fully mature, for sweet, crisp 'baby' carrots. Carrots mature 12–16 weeks after sowing, depending on variety.

PROBLEMS

Carrot root fly can be a serious problem. The best protection is to use barrier methods, either covering the developing crop with horticultural fleece or erecting a barrier a couple of feet high around the entire crop. The female flies only fly a few centimetres off the ground and this will prevent them reaching the crop. If the flies are a problem in your area, it is better to sow carrots widely spaced to avoid the need to thin as this can attract the flies.

COMPANIONS

Inter-cropping carrots with onions, leeks or chives is said to deter carrot root fly. Other good companions are rosemary, sage and scorzonera.

▦ PARSNIP *Pastinaca sativa*

Popular winter root crops, parsnips are slow-growing and will grow in fairly poor soil, although they will give a better crop in fertile soil.

GROWING AND HARVESTING

Sow in mid-spring, three seeds per station, about 15–30cm (6–12in) apart, and thin to the strongest seedling once they have emerged. Plants will take about five months to mature. Keep the water supply fairly constant to prevent the roots cracking.

Parsnips are very hardy and you can leave the plants in the ground all winter to save you the trouble of storing them, simply pulling up a few as needed. Come spring, any left unused grow again and if left the flowers will attract beneficial insects.

PROBLEMS

Parsnips suffer from canker, which can erode the roots and cause deep brown fissures. Grow resistant varieties such as 'Avonresister', and mulch the crowns with well-rotted compost to stop them cracking and drying out. Apply lime if your soil is acid. Parsnips are also affected by carrot root fly.

COMPANIONS

As for carrots.

▦ CELERY *Apium graveolens*

There are two schools of thought among celery lovers. One says that unless you blanch the stems celery is not worth eating. The other holds that the so-called 'self-blanching' varieties make this unnecessary – and as you can pull just a few stalks as you need them, unblanched celery gives a crop for much longer. The leaves can be used to flavour stews and casseroles.

GROWING AND HARVESTING

Sow seed indoors in trays in late winter. Prick out seedlings singly, grow on and harden off for planting out in early summer. Put self-blanching varieties about 23cm (9in) apart. The bed should be as rich as possible and the plants grown as fast as possible or the stalks will be tough and stringy. Mulch and water lavishly: the plants are shallow-rooted and must never suffer drought. A side dressing or two of manure will not go amiss. The traditional method for white celery is to plant about

LEFT: *The red stalked 'Ruby Chard' makes a decorative addition to the vegetable garden. Here it is with strawberries.* CENTRE: *Climbing beans are usually grown up teepees of long, thin poles (beanpoles) which are easily relocated when you rotate your crops, but they can also be grown on a chicken-wire trellis.* RIGHT: *Bush beans need no support if grown close together.*

30cm (12in) apart in a trench about 25cm (10in) deep. About three weeks before harvest, tie the plants into tight bunches, wrapping them with cardboard or thick paper to prevent soil getting between the stalks, and fill the trench with soil so only the leaves show and the stalks are kept in the dark. This is, however, a lot of trouble and increases the risk of celery leaf-spot disease.

There is a short cut. Plant on an ordinary level bed and, again three weeks before harvest, bundle up the plants with black plastic, leaving the leaves uncovered. This has the advantage that you can do just a couple of plants at a time, but you need to be vigilant that snails do not get into the parcels.

Green celery lovers only have to wait for the plants to mature (about three months from seedlings, five months from seed) and then they pull outside stalks as needed, taking the rest of the plant before it starts to flower. With white celery, harvest the entire plant at once; it is also best to harvest all the plants at the one time.

PROBLEMS

Celery can suffer from celery fly and celery leaf spot. Remove affected leaves and burn them. If necessary spray with Bordeaux mixture (see page 85). Most celery seed is treated with a fungicide, but this is not organic. Celery can also suffer from slug damage.

COMPANIONS

Leeks, tomatoes and dwarf beans.

CELERIAC

Apium graveolens rapaceum

Celeriac is hardier, more disease-resistant and easier to grow than celery, but needs a long growing season. Prepare ground with a green manure crop of vetch.

GROWING AND HARVESTING

Celeriac prefers a sunny position in rich, water-retentive soil. Sow under cover in spring, harden off and plant out in late spring or early summer about 30cm (12in) apart. Keep well-watered to prevent any check to growth. Lift the globe-shaped swollen stems from mid to late autumn.

PROBLEMS
See celery – but celeriac is generally trouble-free.

COMPANIONS
Leeks, onions and runner beans.

ALLIACEAE

ONION *Allium cepa*
Use both early and late varieties and store carefully for a year-round supply. Onions are useful for inter-cropping as well as for a main crop.

GROWING AND HARVESTING
Onions need a good rich soil, so prepare the bed with a thick dressing of well-rotted manure or compost. Add lime to raise the pH above 6.5. Sets are the easiest way to grow onions, and these can be planted in spring about 5–10cm (2–4in) apart. Set them so the tips are just below ground level, so the birds will not pull them out. Seed can be sown in shallow drills in early spring, and then thinned to a similar spacing to sets. Make sure they have a

Garlic can be grown either as a crop in the vegetable garden or as a companion plant amongst flowers and fruit. It is said to be beneficial when grown with roses.

regular and even supply of water while they grow. The bulbs will be ready to lift when the foliage withers and turns brown. Lift the bulbs and leave them in the sun for a few days to dry off completely or they may rot in storage. Always keep onions in a dry, well-ventilated, frost-free place.

PROBLEMS
Watch for onion fly, which looks like a small black version of the aphids that attack roses. They are attracted by the onion scent, which is strongest when the seedlings are thinned. Help to avoid problems by sowing thinly or growing from sets.

If you see signs of rot, remove and burn the affected plants, and avoid growing onions on the same plot for several years. Reduce the likelihood of such problems by not over-feeding and not bending over the tops to induce ripening.

COMPANIONS
Onions grow well with carrots, lettuce, beets, chamomile and summer savory. Do not grow with beans as they inhibit each other's growth.

VARIETIES
Shallots are smaller and milder in flavour than main crop onions. They are easy to grow from sets and can be harvested earlier. Japanese onion varieties can be sown in August to ripen the following June, before the main crop varieties. Small salad or spring onions have a milder flavour. They are quicker maturing but do not store well, so sow them at regular intervals from early spring to summer for successional crops.

GARLIC *Allium sativum*
Most of us think of garlic as a seasoning to be used sparingly, but fresh garlic can be served up lavishly as long as the sulphur is well cooked out of it.

GROWING AND HARVESTING
Garlic is very easy to grow, provided you give it a sunny site. Start by buying a few bulbs at the greengrocer's either in autumn or in early spring,

breaking them up into cloves and planting the cloves about 15cm (6in) apart. The soil should be good, although it need not be extravagantly so, and the plants should be well-watered while they are growing. When the foliage begins to die down in autumn, you can lift the bulbs and hang them in the kitchen to dry, keeping the biggest and best for next season's planting.

PROBLEMS
Garlic is generally trouble-free.

COMPANIONS
Garlic is widely used as a companion crop for other plants to help against a variety of pests and diseases, but do not grow it with peas or beans as it inhibits their growth.

▬ LEEK *Allium porrum*
A hardy winter vegetable, leeks are an easy crop to grow as long as you give them a rich, moist soil.

GROWING AND HARVESTING
For an early crop, sow seeds in gentle heat in January or February, otherwise sow in a seedbed outdoors in spring. Transplant the seedlings to their cropping position when they are fairly large, about 20cm (8in) tall. Shorten the tops by about a half and cut back extra-long roots. Make holes about 15cm (6in) deep with a dibber and drop a young leek in each. Do not refill the holes but allow watering to wash the soil into the hole as the plants grow, in order to blanch the lower part of the plant – it is the white part that is so delicious. The richer the soil, the fatter the leeks will be, and a boost of liquid manure every three weeks or so will keep them growing quickly.

Leeks take about 30 weeks to produce large stems, but tasty young leeks can be cropped earlier. Fully mature plants can be left in the ground until required.

PROBLEMS
Leeks are generally healthy and trouble-free. Sometimes they can be attacked by onion fly, but

The red leaves of the lettuce 'Lollo Rosso' make a decorative border in the vegetable garden or in the ornamental garden. They also create a splash of colour in a summer leaf salad.

pyrethrum is an effective remedy (see page 81). If onion thrips appear, hose them off.

COMPANIONS
Leeks and carrots are mutually beneficial – leeks deter carrot fly and carrots aid the growth of leeks. Leeks also do well with onions and celery.

CHENOPODIACEAE

▬ BEETROOT *Beta vulgaris*
The colourful swollen roots can be eaten in summer salads or stored for winter use.

GROWING AND HARVESTING
Give beetroot a deep, well-drained soil enriched with plenty of organic matter. The earliest sowings can be made under cloches in early spring, and sowing can continue at intervals until mid-summer. Put them in shallow drills about 2.5cm (1in) deep and 10cm (4in) apart. Mulch beds and keep well-

watered. Pull alternate roots when they are golf-ball size, leaving the rest to mature. Lift main crops at about tennis-ball size, before they become woody.

PROBLEMS
Generally trouble-free, but mildew may be a problem.

COMPANIONS
Onions, kohlrabi and dwarf beans.

▨ SWISS CHARD
Beta vulgaris var. *cicla*
A member of the beetroot family, this is an easy to grow vegetable for its large crop of leaves on fleshy stalks, and it is often used as a spinach substitute.

GROWING AND HARVESTING
Swiss chard crops over a long season and two sowings, in April and July, will give an almost year-round supply. Put the seeds 2.5cm (1in) deep and about 45cm (18in) apart, in a rich, moisture-retentive soil. Add lime if the soil is acid. Chard will wilt in hot conditions unless you keep it constantly watered, and if it is allowed to dry out too often it will run to flower, which finishes the crop. In autumn, cover plants with cloches to keep plants growing for cropping over winter. You can start harvesting when the plants have half a dozen good-sized leaves, by just gently breaking off a couple of the outside ones. As long as you leave each plant at least four or five leaves, you should have an almost constant harvest for several months.

PROBLEMS
Slugs and snails are the most likely worry.

COMPANIONS
Similar to beetroot.

VARIETIES
'Ruby Chard' has red stems and is pretty enough to plant in the flower bed; the red fades out in the cooking and the flavour is the same. 'Rainbow Chard' has red, purple, yellow or white stalks.

▨ SPINACH *Spinacea oleracea*
Spinach is easy to grow, very nutritious and can be cropped throughout the year.

GROWING AND HARVESTING
It can be grown just like Swiss chard, except the plants do not crop for as long and successional sowings should be made every few weeks.

OTHER FAMILIES

▨ LETTUCE *Lactuca sativa*
Lettuces come in a great variety of shapes and colours, from long green cos to crisp icebergs and red and green loose-leafed types. They are all ideal for inter-planting between slower-growing crops.

GROWING AND HARVESTING
A lettuce grown at speed will always be crisper and tastier than one grown sluggishly. This means rich soil, mulch to keep the roots cool and regular watering. If the plants dry out, growth will be checked and the plants will take that as permission to flower. You can have lettuce most of the year if you sow every three or four weeks, starting in early spring and finishing in autumn. Sow in shade in summer, as the seed will not germinate in high temperatures. Sow thinly in drills, about 1.25cm (1/2in) deep, thinning the seedlings progressively. Do not waste the thinnings – add them to salads.

Estimate 8–14 weeks from sowing to harvest. With firm hearting types, cut the whole plant when you judge it big enough: the loose leaf and radicchio types can be cut whole or taken leaf by leaf as needed. For perfect crispness, water the day before.

PROBLEMS
Deal with aphids and slugs in the usual way. Botrytis or downy mildew may be a problem in cool, damp conditions. Remove affected plants.

COMPANIONS
Carrots, radishes and strawberries. Growing chervil nearby is said to reduce problems with aphids.

▬▬ SWEET CORN *Zea mays*

Sweet corn is best eaten freshly picked, as the sugar starts to turn to starch when cut. The newer hybrid extra sweet varieties should not be grown with other varieties as they are less sweet when cross-pollinated.

GROWING AND HARVESTING

Corn loves a long, warm summer and a rich soil. American Indians used to plant a fish beneath each plant to feed it; today we prefer a handful of blood and bone. Sow the seeds under glass in spring, or outdoors once the soil has warmed up in late spring. Plant in blocks, which gives more effective pollination than planting in rows. Mound up soil around the base of the plant to support the tall stems. Mulch around plants with well-rotted compost or manure and ensure they have plenty of water when flowering and when the cobs start to swell. The corn is ready when the 'silks' turn brown – test by scratching a kernel or two with your thumbnail and seeing if it bleeds a milky juice.

PROBLEMS

Generally trouble-free.

COMPANIONS

Grows well with dill, potatoes, peas and beans – runner beans can even be grown up the corn plants.

▬▬ ASPARAGUS *Asparagus officinalis*

Asparagus has a reputation for being difficult. It is not, but it does need patience, fertile soil and, for preference, a rather sandy soil.

GROWING AND HARVESTING

You can start asparagus from seed sown in spring in a nursery bed or by buying one- or two-year-old crowns. Choose the biggest crowns. Males produce more, fatter spears and do not spread seed all over the garden. (Replace any that show red berries – they are females.) Asparagus likes rich soil and you should prepare the bed with plenty of compost or rotted manure. Dig a trench 30cm (12in) wide and 20cm (8in) deep, with the centre slightly raised. Set

This asparagus is at the end of its cutting season, when the spears have developed into ferny leaf stems. Leave the last few shoots on the plant to make foliage.

the crowns along the raised section, 30–40cm (15–20in) apart, with their roots well spread. Cover, and keep well-watered. Begin to cut spears in the second year. Cut every couple of days for about two weeks, leaving the later shoots to make foliage to keep the plants going. It takes four to five years for the plants to get big enough to cope with a full cutting season of eight weeks. Follow with a light dressing of blood and bone or liquid manure, and in autumn a layer of well-rotted mulch, to build them back up for next year. After eight to ten years, start a new bed and once it is in full production, dig up the old one.

PROBLEMS

Asparagus beetle can strip the foliage and even kill the plant. Treat with derris. If asparagus rust is seen, remove and burn affected shoots immediately. If necessary, spray with a copper fungicide fortnightly.

COMPANIONS

Asparagus grows well with tomatoes and parsley.

ORGANIC
HERBS

HERBS CAN BE USED CONFIDENTLY IN COOKING WHEN
YOU KNOW THEY HAVE BEEN GROWN ORGANICALLY

Like vegetables, herbs are usually grown for use in the kitchen. Any cook knows how useful it is to have some herbs to hand, and it is a definite benefit to know they have been grown without the use of toxic chemicals. But this is not the only reason to grow them. Many herbs are attractive plants in their own right and can be used in the flower borders as well as the traditional herb garden. Low-growing herbs, such as feverfew, chives or a variety of thymes, will look good at the front of the border, while taller herbs, such as the feathery-leaved fennel, add height and presence to the back of the border. Some, such as pot marigold or chives, have decorative flowers while others, such as the variegated sages and balms, have attractive leaves that will add colour to a border all season long. Many herbs have delightfully aromatic foliage, so plant them along paths or near seating areas, where you can fully enjoy their fragrance.

Many are good companion plants too (see pages 86–9), stimulating the growth of nearby plants, attracting pollinators and other beneficial insects or deterring pests and diseases. For this reason, herbs are worth growing in the vegetable garden, too, amongst the rows or blocks of crops, or as decorative as well as useful edging around the beds.

GROWING HERBS

While there are a lot of different herbs, they do not differ much in their needs. Give them sun and a well-drained soil and do not starve them (but do not over-feed them either – the flavour and scent is stronger if the growth is not over-luxuriant). An annual mulch of light organic matter will benefit most herbs, as well as helping to keep the weeds down. Water them in dry weather when necessary, especially the annual herbs, but you will find that most are fairly drought-resistant. The main exceptions to the general rule are mint *(Mentha* sps), bergamot *(Monarda didyma)* and balm *(Melissa officinalis)*, which like a moist spot. Herbs are generally trouble-free and few have any pest and disease problems. (In fact, homemade herbal infusions were used as sprays against pests and diseases in the past, but these are now illegal.)

Most herbs are easy to grow but some can become a bit scruffy as summer progresses, which is why they were traditionally planted in formal gardens, the patterns imposing order on their waywardness. If you do not pick frequently enough to keep them tidy, they will benefit from cutting back during the summer, unless you are planning to harvest the seedheads – but do not waste the trimmings as they are valuable additions to the compost heap.

The range of herbs you choose will depend on your personal preferences and whether you are growing them for the kitchen, for decoration or as companion plants in the flower or vegetable garden. If growing them for culinary use, it is best to site your herb bed with easy access from the kitchen, to make sure the plants are easy to reach without treading on the border or disturbing other plants, and to grow more than one of each so that you do not harvest favourite plants to death.

Half-hardy annuals, such as the basils and sweet marjoram, should be sown under glass each spring and planted out in fertile soil in a sunny spot once the danger of frost has passed. Make sure they have sufficient water in dry weather. Hardy annuals and biennials, such as angelica, borage, coriander, dill, parsley and so on, will benefit from a reasonably fertile soil and regular watering. Many annuals, such as pot marigold, will self-seed quite freely, popping up around the garden each year.

There are lots of herbaceous perennials to choose from: chives, fennel, lemon balm, lovage, marjoram, mint, oregano and tarragon to name but a few of the most popular. Many are decorative enough for the border, but some need to be controlled. Mints are particularly well-known for being invasive, and need to have their roots contained. Either grow them in a pot, or sink a barrier into the ground around them – anything from an old bucket or a layer of thick plastic to slabs of slate.

Shrubby evergreens, such as hyssop, lavender, rosemary and thyme, need a permanent site in a sunny position with a light, well-drained soil, and make decorative additions to any border. More tender plants, such as lemon verbena, can be grown in containers and moved to a frost-free position in a greenhouse or conservatory over winter. Bay trees will survive outside in winter, but in very bad weather they do benefit from some protection.

These two herbs, angelica (left) and fennel (above) will make a striking addition to a mixed border and also attract beneficial insects to the garden. The architectural heads of angelica are ideal for the back of the border, and the feathery foliage of the fennel makes an attractive background for flower displays. Be sure to remove the seedheads of both before they self-seed.

ORGANICALLY GROWN
FRUIT

IT IS NOT DIFFICULT TO GROW
DELICIOUS FRUIT ORGANICALLY

THE HOME ORCHARD

No one with childhood memories of picking fruit from their own trees will consider a garden complete without at least one fruit tree. A fruit tree will be with you for many years so select the best. There is no need to confine your choice to the standard commercial cultivars, although these may be the easiest to find. The commercial grower needs cast-iron fruit that look uniform, travel well and will not get damaged in the rough handling of the market, and the bigger the crop the better. Gardeners can handle the fruit gently and do not need a crop bigger than the family can eat. We can concentrate on the old-fashioned varieties that offer the finest flavour.

Few of us are fortunate enough to have room for a large orchard, so we need to choose carefully, but there should be room for fruit in even the smallest garden. Both fruit and fruit blossom are decorative enough for the ornamental garden, and most trees can be trained to grow against walls and fences and in small spaces, for example, as cordons or fans.

Always buy the best plants available; you will find that a specialist grower offers the best choice and the most helpful advice. Visit the nursery, if possible, to select top-quality plants, whether they are bare-rooted or container-grown. Look for trees with a good general shape with well-positioned branches and a good root system. Young plants should establish quicker and crop earlier. Avoid trees that have obviously been grown in containers for several years as these will not establish as well.

Trees are grafted on to different rootstocks, which will affect their vigour and the eventual size of the plant, and you need to select the appropriate one for your garden (see Rootstocks, page 43). Check the graft union will be high enough above ground level to prevent the top part (scion) growing its own roots.

Some fruit varieties are self-fertile, but many need cross-pollination with another variety, or sometimes two, to give a good crop, so pick a selection of varieties that will flower at the same time. There are early, mid-season and late-flowering varieties for most fruits. Avoid the early ones if frost is a problem in your area, as frost will damage the blossoms and you could lose your crop.

Bear in mind, too, the season of cropping and the keeping qualities of the fruit in making your choice.

CLOCKWISE, FROM TOP LEFT:
Cherries can be bright red or as black as plums: it depends on variety. • Apples can be grown in the smallest of gardens if trained as cordons or fans. • The nectarine is only a smooth-skinned peach, though the flavour is subtly different. • The 'Conference' pear offers fine flavour and heavy crops.

If you have room for several trees, aim for a range of cropping times to extend the season.

Check the trees carefully for any signs of pests and diseases and to be sure that they are vigorous and growing well. Some fruit are covered by health schemes; buy only trees certified free from disease.

ROOTSTOCKS

When you buy a tree, you are in most cases buying two trees grafted together. The top, or scion, gives you the variety; the bottom, or rootstock, determines the vigour and eventual size. Rootstocks vary from the very vigorous, which will give you a large tree, to semi-dwarfing and dwarfing, which are suitable for bushes, pyramids and trained forms such as espaliers and fans; and the very dwarfing, which are suitable for small bushes, cordons and container plants. Your local nursery will be able to advise on appropriate types.

PLANTING

Give any fruit tree the best of everything – which means sunshine, good drainage, and good, well-dug soil. Avoid windy sites as wind can damage growth and cause fruit to fall, and frost pockets as fruit blossom is very sensitive to frost damage.

Most bare-rooted fruit trees are best planted in early winter, though container-grown trees can be planted at any time of year. Before you plant, prepare the spot as well as you would the vegetable patch and, if you are planting a tree in the lawn, keep a mulched, grass-free bed a metre or more wide around it for at least four or five years.

You will need a stake for all but the very dwarfing forms. If you are growing trained fruit which require support, erect a system of posts and wires before planting to avoid any disturbance to the new trees. If you are growing fruit against a wall, where the soil may be dry and possibly less fertile, prepare the ground well, digging in lots of organic matter. Position the tree at least 30cm (12in) out, spreading the roots away from the wall, and make sure the tree is kept well fed and watered at all times.

CONTINUING CARE

We make outrageous demands on our fruit trees, expecting them to bear unnaturally large crops of large and succulent fruit, and so we need to keep them growing steadily with a mulch of well-rotted manure or compost every spring. This should be sufficient fertilizer; once trees are mature it is not advisable to encourage them to make lush growth at the expense of fruit. Water well in dry spells, especially when the fruit is forming.

Thinning crops, removing from a third to a half of the immature fruit, is usually recommended. It is an optional procedure and it does seem perverse, but there are benefits. You get larger individual fruit, and rots and fungi will have a hard time spreading, and it evens out the workload on the tree, so that it does not fruit itself into exhaustion one year and take the following year off. Heavily laden trees will naturally drop some fruit in mid-summer, so delay thinning until after this.

PRUNING AND TRAINING

Prune to remove any damaged or diseased wood and crossing branches and to create an open framework. With apples and pears this can be done in winter, but with trees such as plums and cherries, which are susceptible to silver leaf, prune in summer instead.

By pruning and shaping during the first few years of growth, fruit trees can be trained into a variety of shapes: fans, espaliers and so on, so that they can be grown in restricted spaces. Continued regular pruning will be needed to maintain the shape and keep the tree cropping regularly.

When pruning always use sharp, clean secateurs; cut back to a point just above a bud and make a clean cut. Remember that the branch will grow out in the direction the bud is facing.

COMPANIONS

Try nasturtiums under trees to keep away woolly aphids, southernwood to repel fruit tree moths, and tansy to keep away harmful flying insects. Chives

This fan-trained pear benefits from the shelter of a warm wall. A decorative edging of Sweet William adds colour through the spring and summer months.

are said to increase the health of apples and prevent apple scab. Other good companions are stinging nettles, garlic and horseradish.

PROBLEMS

A fruit tree will be better able to resist pests and diseases if it is flourishing in healthy soil in a climate that suits it. Good hygiene is an important preventive, removing fallen fruit and leaves promptly, and cutting out any dead or damaged branches.

▬▬ APPLE *Malus domestica*

Beautiful in blossom and generous in fruit, the apple is best loved of all the tree fruit. Apples can be grown as standards or bushes, or trained in various ways, including cordons, fans, espaliers and stepovers, so it should be possible to find room for them in even the smallest garden. To give a full crop, trees need to be pollinated by a different variety, so you need at least two – and do not forget to check that the ones you choose will blossom at the same time.

GROWING AND HARVESTING

Plant bare-rooted trees in early winter. They do best in a sunny, sheltered site. Follow the general growing instructions on page 43.

Pick fruit when fully ripe. Lift the fruit and gently twist; it will come away easily if it is ripe. Pick carefully to avoid bruising, and only store perfect fruit. Keep them in a cool, dry, frost-free place and check them regularly, removing any that show signs of rotting. Windfall apples will not keep.

PROBLEMS

Although the list of possible problems is a long one, if you keep your trees flourishing, with an annual mulch of compost and watering in dry weather, you should have little trouble. Aphids may appear on young shoots. See page 82 for general treatments. Woolly aphids cover themselves with a white waxy coating which protects them from sprays. Simply scrape them off the plant or paint them with methylated spirits. Cut out large infestations.

The codling moth lays its eggs on developing fruit so little caterpillars can burrow inside and eat the core. Reduce the problem by hanging pheromone traps in the trees from late spring to late summer. If this is not sufficient, spray with derris.

Apple sawfly damage is similar to that caused by the codling moth, but affects the fruit earlier in the season, and can leave a characteristic ribbon-like scar. The fruits fail to ripen and fall early. Destroy infected fruits and, if severe, spray the tree with derris.

Tie greasebands around trees, leaving them in place from autumn to spring, to prevent winter moths crawling up the trees to lay their eggs.

Fungus diseases, such as mildew on the young leaves and scab, which makes black blotches on the leaves and fruit, can occur. Remove all affected material, and sweep up fallen leaves on which the fungus could overwinter. Inspect regularly for signs of canker, which cause sunken, wrinkled discoloured patches, and cut out any diseased wood.

Try to select varieties that are resistant to recurrent problems in your garden, such as 'Sunset', which is resistant to scab and powdery mildew, and 'Newton's Wonder', which is resistant to canker.

▨ CHERRY *Prunus avium, P. cerasus*

Cherries are as popular with the birds as with us and it can be a challenge to get the crop before they do. Sweet cherries *(P. avium)* are vigorous and can grow very large, so to protect the trees from the birds grow them on a dwarfing rootstock, or as fans trained against a south-facing wall. Acid cherries *(P. cerasus)* are not as strong growing, and can be grown as a fan against a north-facing wall. If you only have room for one cherry, choose a self-fertile variety, or you will need at least two to be sure of a crop.

GROWING AND HARVESTING

Cherry trees like a deep, rich, well-drained soil and shelter from strong wind. Sweet cherries prefer a sunny site, while the acid ones will do well in shade. Cherries should be picked when they are ripe but before they go soft – or the birds will get them. They do not store for long.

To protect apples from codling moth damage, hang pheromone traps in the trees to catch the male moths.

PROBLEMS

Birds always seem to devour sweet cherries the day before you plan to pick them, therefore the crop is best kept under a net if possible. Cherries are prone to both bacterial canker and silver leaf, so avoid winter pruning, cut out affected branches, and if necessary treat with Bordeaux mixture (see page 85). Cherry blackfly can be treated with insecticidal soap. Trap winter moths with greasebands.

▨ FIG *Ficus carica*

Figs can grow very large but will not produce a good crop of fruit unless their roots are restricted.

GROWING AND HARVESTING

Figs need a warm sunny position to crop well, and do best trained against a south-facing wall, or in a greenhouse. Dig out a planting area about 1m (3¹/₄ft) square. Fill the base of the hole with rubble and line with paving slabs or other impenetrable material to restrict their roots. Fill in with a mix of soil and well-rotted organic material. Do not give figs too rich a soil or they will make leafy growth at the expense of fruit. Water well in dry weather, thin in summer, and protect from frost in winter.

Figs are ripe when they change colour, turn soft and hang downwards. They can only be stored if they have been dried or frozen.

PROBLEMS

Birds love fresh figs, so netting may be necessary. Watch out for botrytis and canker and remove any infected material as soon as seen.

▬▬ PEACHES AND NECTARINES

Prunus persica

These delicious fruit will crop in temperate climates, as long as they are given a sunny sheltered position, preferably against a south-facing wall. They are both grown in the same way; the only real difference between them is that peaches have furry skins while nectarines have smooth skins, and nectarines are slightly more tender.

GROWING AND HARVESTING

They like a deep, fertile, well-drained soil, so prepare the ground well, and give an annual mulch of well-rotted compost or manure. Peaches are self-fertile, but flower early and may need protection from frost and pollination by hand. Peaches fruit on young wood produced the previous year, so careful pruning in early spring and summer is important to produce a good crop. To obtain a crop of good-sized fruit, thin in early summer.

The fruit are ripe when they come away easily when gently lifted. Handle with care as they bruise easily. They will only keep for a few days but if you have a large crop they can be bottled.

PROBLEMS

The main problems are aphids, red spider mite and peach leaf curl. Leaf curl causes red blisters on the leaves followed by white spores, and the leaves fall early. Remove all infected leaves as soon as you see them. In winter spray with copper fungicide and repeat after 10–14 days. Spray again in autumn before the annual leaf fall.

▬▬ PEAR   *Pyrus communis*

In general, pears require more warmth and sunshine than apples to produce the best crops. Pears need pollinating by a different variety so you will need to grow at least two types that flower at the same time.

GROWING AND HARVESTING

See general growing information on page 43. Do not leave pears to ripen fully on the tree but pick while they are still firm, otherwise they may become overripe and soft and mushy in the centre. Store them in a cool place to ripen – preferably laid out on shelves, each wrapped in tissue paper. Late varieties can be left on the tree longer.

PROBLEMS

Pears suffer from the same problems as apples though are generally a little less bothered by them.

▬▬ PLUM   *Prunus domestica*

Plums, greengages and damsons are vigorous trees which can produce a large crop of fruit, although they can also be grown on dwarfing rootstocks as pyramids or fans. They can be irregular in cropping because the flowers are susceptible to frost damage.

GROWING AND HARVESTING

They like a rich, well-drained soil and a sheltered site where there is least risk of frost damage. Plums take several years to start cropping. In a good year heavy crops can break branches and result in poorly flavoured fruit, and can exhaust the plant so that cropping is poor the following year; so thin in summer, leaving the fruits about 5–8cm (2–3in) apart. Avoid pruning in winter as they are susceptible to silver leaf disease. Plums grown as free-standing trees should not need pruning.

Plums for eating are best picked when fully ripe but not yet soft. Plums for preserving should be picked slightly early.

PROBLEMS

Birds and wasps can cause significant damage to crops. A particular problem is silver leaf disease, a fungus that infects the tree through pruning cuts in winter. The leaves develop a silvery appearance and the branches die back. Brown stains can be seen in the wood. To avoid infection, do not prune in winter, and disinfect your tools after you do prune. If symptoms appear, cut back and burn infected growth.

SOFT FRUIT

While not all gardens can give a lot of space to tree fruit, soft fruit are ideal for the smaller garden. With careful choice of varieties it is possible to have delicious fruit from late spring to early autumn, but the birds love the fruit too; you will need to net the plants to prevent the birds getting to the crops first.

BLACKCURRANT *Ribes nigrum*

Blackcurrants are easy to grow and the fruit is rich in vitamin C, but the flavour can be rather sharp. Although they are self-fertile, grow several varieties if you have room to spread the cropping season.

GROWING AND HARVESTING

Blackcurrants are grown as free-standing bushes, pruned to form stools, and need no support or training. They like a rich soil and sunny conditions to give a good crop, and are gross feeders; so as well as preparing the ground well, give them a good mulch of well-rotted manure or compost each spring and a couple of handfuls of blood, fish and bone. They fruit best on one-year-old growth, so in late summer cut fruited wood back to ground level.

Pick the fruit as soon as they are ripe to avoid the birds getting to them first.

PROBLEMS

Big bud mite can be a serious problem. Tiny mites attack the buds in early summer, causing them to swell. Pick off any big round buds that you notice and burn them. However, the mites carry the reversion virus which is more of a problem. Bushes lose vigour and yield is reduced. Dig up affected bushes and plant new ones elsewhere in the garden.

Blackcurrants can be affected by mildew or leaf spot; pick off and burn affected leaves as soon as seen. If sawfly are a problem, pick off caterpillars and, if necessary, spray with derris or pyrethrum.

COMPANIONS

Nettles are said to increase the keeping qualities of the fruit and attract beneficial insects to keep pests down.

CURRANT, RED AND WHITE
Ribes sps

These are usually grown as open-centred bushes on a short stem or cordon. They are not troubled by reversion and are long-lived and highly productive.

GROWING AND HARVESTING

They do not need as rich conditions as blackcurrants, and although they prefer a sunny position, they will tolerate some shade, and will even fruit when grown

LEFT: *Blackcurrants are grown as free-standing bushes, and although they take up quite a bit of room they are well worth growing as the fruits are rich in vitamin C.* RIGHT: *Gooseberries can be grown on even the smallest plot of land as they are easily trained as cordons.*

against a north-facing wall. Give them shelter from frost and strong winds. They need plenty of potash, and will benefit from an application of rock potash. Prune to form an open cup-shaped bush, or cordons.

Pick sprigs rather than individual fruit, as they are small and easily squashed. Although they last well, pick them quickly or the birds will get to them.

PROBLEMS

They are much loved by birds. Aphids, sawfly, mildew and leaf spot can also be problems.

▨ GOOSEBERRY *Ribes grossularia*

Once enormously popular, with specialist gooseberry clubs and over 3,000 varieties named over the years, gooseberries are easy to grow and train.

GROWING AND HARVESTING

Gooseberries prefer a sunny position but tolerate partial shade. Avoid cold areas and frost pockets, as they flower early and the flowers can be damaged by frosts. Give them a good, well-drained soil. If the soil is sandy and dry, work in plenty of organic matter or they may not grow and yield well. They need lots of potash so give them an application of rock potash in spring. Apply an annual mulch of well-rotted manure or compost, which will also help to keep the soil moist – and reduce the need to weed under these prickly bushes.

Gooseberries respond well to training and are best grown as open-centred, goblet-shaped bushes or cordons. Once the shape is established, prune to encourage the fruiting spurs which develop on older wood. Early thinnings can be picked when green and used in cooking, leaving the rest to ripen fully.

PROBLEMS

American gooseberry mildew can affect leaves, shoots and fruit, covering them with a white powdery coating. Good cultivation and growing resistant varieties is the best preventive. Sulphur-based sprays can help – but not on 'sulphur-shy' varieties. Gooseberry sawfly caterpillars can rapidly strip a plant's leaves. Be vigilant and remove eggs

and caterpillars as soon as you spot them. As a last resort, spray with derris or pyrethrum (see page 85). Aphids and leaf spot may also be problems.

COMPANIONS

Tomatoes are reputed to aid their growth.

▨ RASPBERRY *Rubus idaeus*

Good crops for a cool climate, raspberries are an easy crop to grow and will give good yields. Blackberries and hybrid berries are grown in a similar way.

GROWING AND HARVESTING

Give raspberries a site sheltered from strong winds. A sunny position is best, though they will tolerate partial shade. (Autumn-fruiting varieties need full sun.) They do best in a rich, well-drained but moisture-retentive soil. Set the young plants about 45cm (18in) apart in soil lavishly prepared, and mulch every spring. The best way to grow them is to train them along a system of posts and wires, pruning them by cutting the just-fruited canes right to the ground after harvest to make way for new ones that will bear next year's crop.

The fruit is most delicious when allowed to ripen on the bush. For freezing pick a day or two earlier.

PROBLEMS

Cane spot makes purplish spots on the canes and stunts them; blight can cause the canes to wither and die back. Remove and burn affected canes and spray with Bordeaux mixture (see page 85), or grow resistant varieties elsewhere in the garden.

The larvae of the raspberry beetle feed on the developing fruit, distorting them. In winter, remove mulches and cultivate around the canes to bring the pupae to the surface where birds will eat them. If the problem is serious, spray with derris (see page 81) after flowering. Raspberries can also be affected by mildews and aphids. Birds love the fruit so you will need to net the crop.

COMPANIONS

Garlic, marigolds, tansy or strawberries.

Raspberries are easy to grow in cool climates, responding well to organic methods and giving a heavy crop. They appreciate a sunny spot with some shelter from wind.

▬▬ STRAWBERRY *Fragaria* x *ananassa*

You can find room for a crop of strawberries in any garden; they can even be grown without a garden in containers, windowboxes or hanging baskets.

GROWING AND HARVESTING

Start by buying certified virus-free plants in a variety that is best for your local climate. Plant in late summer for a crop the following year. Give them a sunny, sheltered site and a well-drained but moisture-retentive soil. Prepare the site with plenty of well-rotted manure, and add some bonemeal to provide phosphorus. If possible, avoid areas where potatoes, tomatoes and strawberries have been grown recently, to reduce the chance of problems with verticillium wilt and eelworms.

Set the plants about 38–45cm (15–18in) apart, in rows about 60cm (2ft) apart. Set the crowns of the plants at soil level – too deep and they will rot, too shallow and they may dry out – and spread the roots out well. They will not do much until spring, when the first flowers will appear.

It is then time to give them a mulch to keep the fruit clean and the roots cool. Although straw is the traditional mulch, some people now prefer to plant strawberries through a black plastic mulch instead. Cover plants with cloches for earlier crops. By mid-summer the plants will appreciate a little blood and bone. By the time the first fruit ripens, the plants will be producing runners. Allow runners to develop and fruiting will slow down; on the other hand, the runners are an easy way to increase the number of plants.

Keep the fruit picked as it ripens. After fruiting, remove debris and old leaves, cutting the plants back to about 10cm (4in) from the crown.

PROBLEMS

Strawberries can be affected by botrytis and mildew, aphids and red spider mites. Buy certified virus-free stock, and replace plants with new stock every four or five years to avoid virus problems.

COMPANIONS

Borage is the traditional companion for strawberries. Also recommended are lettuce, spinach and beans.

MISCELLANEOUS FRUIT

▬▬ GRAPE *Vitis vinifera*

In a cool, temperate climate most grapes grown outdoors are wine varieties, but a few dessert varieties can be grown in warmer areas, especially if positioned against a sunny, south-facing wall. For a reliable crop of dessert grapes, however, vines are best grown in the greenhouse. Vines are self-fertile, so only one variety is needed.

GROWING AND HARVESTING

Choose an appropriate variety for your area. They are more tolerant of poorer soils than most fruit, as long as they are well-drained, but will benefit from well-prepared ground with generous amounts of organic matter, and an annual mulch of well-rotted compost or manure. Vines fruit on the current season's growth, and are very vigorous, needing hard pruning to control them. They are usually trained against a system of posts and wires.

Cut off bunches of grapes in autumn when the fruit is ripe and fully coloured.

PROBLEMS

Vines can suffer from botrytis and mildews. These problems are aggravated by stagnant air and dry conditions at the root. Reduce problems by careful pruning to keep the plant open and air flowing, and if necessary use a sulphur- or copper-based spray. Alternatively, avoid the problem by replacing with resistant varieties. Keep wasps and birds away from the fruit by netting, or covering individual bunches with paper or net bags.

COMPANIONS

Vines are said to do well growing over mulberry or elm trees. Hyssop, legumes and mustard are also reputed to aid their growth.

RHUBARB *Rheum rhaponticum*

Although technically a vegetable as it is the stems that we eat, rhubarb is often included amongst the fruits as it is eaten as a dessert. Whichever way you look at it, rhubarb is easy to grow. The plants are handsome in their luxuriance, and would make a nice divider between the vegetable plot and the main garden.

GROWING AND HARVESTING

Buy a few crowns and plant them half a metre (20in) apart in a rich, moist bed, in sun or light shade. Give the plants a mulch of compost or old manure early each spring, do not let them flower (the flowers are not interesting) and that is all there is to it. You will have rhubarb growing in your garden for ever.

Let rhubarb plants grow for a year to become properly established. In the second spring, you can start taking off the outside stems, leaving at least half a dozen or so to keep the plants going. Do not try to eat the leaves as they are poisonous, although they can be safely composted. To force early crops, simply cover the crowns with a forcing pot, bottomless bucket, or just a thick layer of straw. For even earlier crops, the crowns can be dug up and brought under cover.

PROBLEMS

Rhubarb is rarely troubled by pests and diseases.

CLOCKWISE, FROM FAR LEFT: *Rhubarb can be blanched by placing a big flower pot over the developing shoots, but naturally grown stalks like these are acceptable.*
• *Strawberry flowers and leaves are pretty enough to use as edgings in the flower garden.*
• *You need to mulch to keep strawberries out of the mud, straw or similar can be used for this purpose.*

EDIBLE FLOWERS

THERE ARE MANY FLOWERS YOU CAN EAT IF THEY HAVE BEEN GROWN ORGANICALLY

Eating flowers (other than artichokes and cauliflowers) may at first seem a bit eccentric to some, but in fact there are many flowers that are edible. You would not want to eat flowers from the florist as you do not know what they might have been sprayed with. However, if you have grown your own without using toxic sprays, you can add a touch of the exotic to your cuisine. Most are eaten fresh, but if you do cook flowers do so very quickly or they will be flavourless and tough.

But before you go out and sample the flowers, remember that many common garden flowers are poisonous – daffodils, lily-of-the-valley, daphne, oleanders, rhododendrons, delphiniums, ranunculi, anemones and foxgloves, to name only a few. If in doubt, assume the flower is inedible.

Add a splash of colour to your salads with decorative chive flowers (left) or nasturtiums (right).

SOME EDIBLE FLOWERS

Here, however, are a few common flowers you can safely eat.
- **Nasturtiums** have edible flowers which, like the leaves, have a spicy, peppery flavour. They are ideal in salads, or as a highly decorative garnish.
- **Calendulas** (English or pot marigolds) have petals in shades of orange that add colour and warm flavour to all sorts of foods. Use them fresh in salads, butters and cheeses, or in cooked dishes such as omelettes, soup and rice dishes.
- **Rose petals** can be used in jams, pies and rose-petal sandwiches, as well as to flavour vinegars, syrups and liqueurs and to make rose petal wine. They can also be crystallized to make a 'sweet'.
- **Daylilies** (*Hemerocallis*) can be sautéed in butter. You will also find them dried in Chinese markets.

- **Pumpkin and squash blossoms** are a delicacy when dipped in batter and fried.
- **Violets and pansies** can be crystallized for decorating cakes and desserts, or for eating as attractively coloured 'sweets'.
- **Dahlia petals** can be added to salads.
- **Borage flowers** can be used to add colour and a cucumber flavour to salads. Freeze them in ice-cubes to use in summer drinks, or crystallize them to decorate cakes and desserts.
- **Chrysanthemum petals** are sometimes used in Japanese cooking.
- **Bergamot petals** can be used to decorate salads.
- **Chive flowers** can be eaten fresh in salads, or made into spectacular herb vinegars or butters.
- **Elderflowers** can be made into cordials, jams and jellies, as well as elderflower wine.
- **Lavender flowers** can be used to flavour sugars, jellies, ice-creams and cheeses. Lavender flowers can also be crystallized to use as decorations on cakes and desserts.
- **Rosemary flowers** are good fresh in salads or as decorations for desserts.
- **Thyme flowers** give a distinctive flavour to honey, vinegars, stuffings and butters, as well as salads. Try lemon thyme or the caraway-flavoured *Thymus herba-barona* as well.

THE ORGANIC
LAWN

IT IS POSSIBLE TO HAVE A LAWN WITHOUT
DEPARTING FROM ORGANIC PRINCIPLES

A lawn is just a large collection of plants – grasses and maybe clover – and like other plants it needs to flourish to be presentable. Grass that is growing strongly is more able to shrug off the (few) pests and diseases that may afflict it, will crowd out many of the weeds that try to take hold and will be better able to withstand the wear and tear we subject it to.

As with any other perennial plant, ensure your lawn is made up of a type of grass that suits your soil and aspect. Most grasses do best in a sunny position, although there are grasses suitable for partially shaded sites. Avoid deeply shaded areas. The best site for a lawn is level, well-drained and fertile, and it is important that the ground should be prepared carefully before sowing or turfing. Incorporate lots of organic matter if you can to encourage the activity of earthworms, who are great allies in the maintenance of a healthy lawn.

Do not, however, allow the lawn to become your master. If you find yourself devoting too much time to the lawn, take a hard look at it. You may decide you have too much grass and the design of the garden would actually benefit from replacing some areas with paving or ground cover plantings.

WATERING

Far too much water applied to lawns goes to waste. It is easy to turn on a sprinkler for a while and get the grass nice and wet, but grass roots are lazy and if you coddle them like this they will stay close to the surface and suffer when the weather turns hot and dry. Then, as bits of grass die off, weeds can take hold as soon as the rain returns. The rule is to water infrequently but to do it thoroughly, so the roots grow deep where the soil does not dry out so fast. It is hard to quantify this: much depends on your soil and the weather, but if you have to water more than once a week, even in dry summers, you are not watering deeply enough. However, if there is a dry summer with restrictions on water use or if you prefer not to water the lawn, it is unlikely to cause permanent harm; the grass might brown off but it will soon recover with the autumn rains.

MOWING

Mowing is a kind of constant harvest, a constant removal of nutrients that the grass has taken from the soil, and you need to return them. The easiest way would be to leave the clippings on the lawn to sift down and decompose. If you are in the habit of mowing two or three times a week in the growing season, taking off only a few millimetres or so each time, this is quite practical, but if you put off the chore until the grass is shaggy the clippings will be too coarse and will not rot properly and you risk the possibility of fungal diseases. You are then better off removing the clippings to the compost heap.

FEEDING

Feed a couple of times a year, using a fertilizer that is rich in nitrogen to encourage luxuriant foliage. You can use blood, fish and bone in early spring, and again in early summer if needed, watering it in lavishly as soon as you spread it to avoid any risk of it burning the grass. Alternatively, water the lawn with a high-nitrogen liquid manure, again turning on the sprinklers afterwards.

Reduce the amount of fertilizer needed by sowing a little clover among the grass. Being a legume, it has the ability to 'fix' nitrogen from the air and some of that will be passed on to the grass as the clover roots wax and wane with the seasons.

GENERAL MAINTENANCE

In a healthy organic lawn, most of the maintenance will be done by the soil organisms, particularly earthworms, which will take down dead material, preventing the build-up of thatch. Their burrows will also aerate the lawn. To encourage their activity, maintain a pH above 5.5 as they do not like acid soil. Deal with wormcasts by brushing them out over the surface of the lawn. If a lawn has been worn and compacted by extensive use, or has been neglected, the usual tasks of aerating, scarifying and top dressing, as appropriate, will help to bring it back into good condition.

If the grass is growing strongly there should be few weeds, but some will inevitably appear. Just dig them out, making sure you get all the root.

Lawn grass can be afflicted with mildew and similar fungi, and these can be best controlled by good drainage and aeration. They can be treated by watering with fungicide, but if the problem recurs it is usually because the grass is not happy with the soil conditions or the position is too shady. Replace it with a more suitable type, or with ground covers.

For a healthy organic lawn (top) be sure to choose a grass that suits the local conditions. Weeds can simply be dug out of a lawn (left) rather than using weedkiller. If this process leaves a hole, fill it with soil or compost. Raking (below) will help to remove any dead grass, moss or other debris that can inhibit healthy growth of the grass.

NATURE AND
NATURAL HARMONY

YOU CAN ENJOY A BEAUTIFUL AND PRODUCTIVE GARDEN WHILE STILL
MAINTAINING A HARMONIOUS RELATIONSHIP WITH THE NATURAL WORLD

The natural world is wonderfully complex and interdependent. When we make a garden we inevitably have a great influence on the creatures that are part of it, not only the plants, insects and animals that we can see about us, but also the tiniest microbes in the soil – creatures that we cannot even see and are scarcely aware are there, but which are an integral part of the complex chain of life.

Nature will create its own balance but the demands we make for fruit and vegetables, for cut flowers, and to create an attractive environment that we can enjoy, disrupts the natural harmony. When using chemical sprays and artificial fertilizers and over-cultivating the land we upset the natural balance even further, often destroying the organisms that maintain a healthy long-term environment in our desire for short-term gains.

Organic gardening is simply a way of working with Nature, rather than against it, to redress the balance in a sustainable manner by using natural processes. Rather than adding artificial fertilizers to replace the fertility that we remove with our crops, which may boost plant growth for a while but can deplete the overall soil fertility in the longer term,

organic gardeners feed the soil with natural recycled materials, providing a reservoir of fertility that the plants can draw on as they need. Rather than spray with the chemical pesticides that frequently kill beneficial creatures as well, organic gardeners, by creating a variety of garden habitats, will create an environment which attracts a range of beneficial wildlife. They aim to build a balanced local eco-system in which no one species is likely to get the upper hand and build up to an unacceptable level.

On a wider scale, recent concerns over issues such as genetically modified organisms, pollution by pesticides, loss of natural habitats such as peat bogs and so forth have led to an increasing public aware-ness of the potential problems created by modern farming and gardening practice, and demands for chemical-free food and a safer environment for our children to grow up in are increasing. We can each play our part in our own personal environment. Working with Nature to create a natural harmony can be a particularly satisfying way of gardening, and by using organic methods you will not only be creating a richer environment but also adding another fascinating dimension to your gardening.

An organic garden can be planned and laid out in any manner, from a casual arrangement as pictured above to the rigidly formal. Organic is a philosophy of gardening, not a style or design: it is working in harmony with nature to create a way of gardening that is both environmentally friendly and sustainable in the long term.

THE ECOLOGY

OF THE GARDEN

HOW PLANTS GROW

A plant draws water from the soil through its roots, and takes in carbon dioxide from the air through the pores in its leaves. It is in the leaves that the fascinating process called photosynthesis occurs. The chlorophyll, which gives the leaves their green colour, can absorb the energy of the sun and convert it to chemical energy in the form of carbohydrates or sugars. In the process carbon dioxide and water are used up and oxygen is released as a by-product. This is the most important chemical reaction on earth, as it is the only process by which organisms can manufacture carbohydrates and so almost all life is ultimately dependent on it.

The plants themselves use the carbohydrates both as fuel for their life process and to build up most of their substance; animals, including humans, derive their food by eating plants. Without the oxygen that is liberated as a by-product of photosynthesis, animals and humans could not live.

There are two consequences that are of great importance to the gardener. The first is that plants need to be given adequate sunlight. Plants that

have evolved in different environments, however, will have adapted to grow best with different levels of light. You cannot expect a plant that loves sun, such as a rose, a dahlia or most vegetables, to grow strong and remain healthy when grown in shade. Conversely, plants that naturally grow in forests, such as camellias or azaleas, will suffer if exposed to the full force of the sun in the garden borders. It is possible to tell whether the plant is happy by the tone of its leaves: a sun-lover in shade will become unnaturally dark green as it steps up chlorophyll production to compensate for the lower light levels; a shade lover will go yellow and the leaves may even die if it is exposed to too much sunlight.

The second consequence is that a plant suffering from drought is not merely 'thirsty', it is 'starving'. It may not actually wilt, but without adequate water in its tissues, it cannot photosynthesise at its normal rate and produce sufficient carbohydrates and so growth will begin to stop. It may even rush into premature flower in a last-ditch effort to make seeds and perpetuate itself before it dies. This is why it is important to ensure that vegetables have sufficient water: a check to their growth can induce them to 'bolt' (run to seed) and spoil the harvest. Lettuce is a prime example; it will rapidly run to seed in dry conditions.

ELEMENTS FROM THE SOIL

While over 90 per cent of a plant's substance is made up from the hydrogen, carbon and oxygen it takes from the air and water, it needs other elements in smaller quantities to sustain life. These it gets from the soil, taking them in via its roots. The most important of these are nitrogen (without which proteins cannot be made), phosphorus and potassium. Some twenty or so others, such as calcium, iron,

magnesium, copper, cobalt, sulphur and boron, are needed in much smaller amounts and thus are called 'trace elements'. The list is not very different from that of the elements in our own bodies, although the exact amounts and proportions differ. This should be no surprise, as life is fundamentally the same, for all its varied manifestations.

The plant can only absorb these elements from the soil when they can be dissolved in water, and that is almost always when they are in the form of simple salts such as nitrates and phosphates – or inorganic compounds, as a chemist would describe them. If the soil does not contain enough of these elements, they can be added in fertilizers, either organic or chemical. It is even possible to grow plants entirely without soil, with their roots in solutions of the appropriate salts, a procedure known as hydroponic gardening or hydroponics. But that is the ultimate in artificiality, comparable

CLOCKWISE, FROM TOP LEFT:
• *Bees flourish in a chemical-free environment.* • *An unused clothesline has been recycled into a grape arbour.* • *The froth amongst the foliage in this pond is the spawn of frogs, useful in the organic garden as they eat insect pests.* • *Valuable fertilizer is taken from the raised duck pond.*

to feeding people intravenously. It is exactly the opposite of organic gardening.

THE CYCLE OF LIFE

Gardeners are inclined to look at plants in isolation but plants do not grow thus. Each plant is a part of the complex web of life we call the environment. Take a trip to a wooded area, and look around you. Here you will see the soil mantled with many plants, from trees to small herbs and grasses, all of them busy photosynthesising and drawing nutrients from the soil. After a time the nutrients are returned to the soil: leaves or whole plants die and fall, or animals (including insects) eat bits of plants, and when they have digested them deposit their dung on the soil – and eventually their own dead bodies. Life burgeons and decays, and from that decay new life rises. This is recycling in its purest and most beautiful form, and all is in perfect balance.

Look carefully at the soil. It is covered with a layer of fallen leaves and such (organic matter) but the layer is not very thick. It is easy to see that the leaves are decaying, but what we do not notice is the multitude of living things that are digesting the organic matter and in their turn adding their own dead bodies to the soil. Ranging from worms and small insects down to microscopic bacteria and fungi, without their presence the recycling process could never occur. These living things exist in large quantities: it has been calculated that their weight in the soil of a forest equals that of the trees above.

HUMUS

The result of the work of all these organisms is the wonderful substance called humus. It is neither solid nor liquid but a sort of black colloid, and it gives fertile soil its dark colour and sweet 'earthy' smell. It sticks to the mineral particles that form the framework of the soil (so to speak), filling in the tiny gaps and lining the bigger ones so that water and dissolved nutrients are held within the structure, to be made available to plants as they are

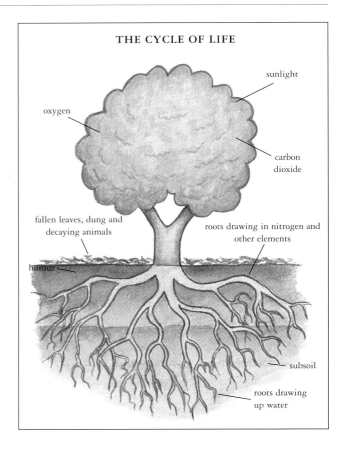

THE CYCLE OF LIFE

sunlight

oxygen

carbon dioxide

fallen leaves, dung and decaying animals

roots drawing in nitrogen and other elements

humus

subsoil

roots drawing up water

needed. Micro-organisms live in the humus, as well as in the coarser matter, and they also yield up nutrients in the form plants can use.

MICRO-ORGANISMS AND PHOSPHORUS

Plants take up phosphorus from the soil, even though the compounds it forms there are all insoluble in water, as the acidic secretions of the micro-organisms dissolve it and make it available to plants. Their activity is timed to the seasons: in winter they are dormant and sluggish and as the weather warms up they step up their activity and give the plants more food just when they need it.

FUNGI

It has been known for a long time that some plants, notably orchids, cannot grow without the presence of certain fungi in the soil around their roots; and it is now believed that this is true of all plants. The fungi live independently in the humus, often showing their presence by mushrooms on the surface, but the plants' roots latch on to them and the tiny threads of the fungus greatly extend the roots' ability to gather moisture and food. Some scientists go so far as to say that without symbiotic relationships with fungi, land plants could never exist and the land would still be barren. Without humus, we cannot really speak of soil – just dirt.

THE IMPORTANCE OF LEGUMES

No living thing can exist without nitrogen, but before chemical fertilizers it was only available to plants and animals as a by-product of life, from the endless recycling of what is called the nitrogen cycle. That it is not a 'closed' cycle is largely due to bacteria that live in nodules on the roots of certain families of plants, most importantly the legumes or pea family. This family includes such familiar species as clover, beans, lupins and many trees and shrubs.

These bacteria have a unique ability – they can 'fix' the nitrogen in the air, combining it with hydrogen and oxygen to form the nitrates and ammonia compounds that plants can take in. When the bacteria die, the legumes absorb these elements, and when they in turn contribute to the humus (or the compost heap) they leave it richer than before. In this way nitrogen becomes available to other plants – and eventually to us.

THE NEED TO REPLACE HUMUS

Humus is not the end. In its turn it is gradually depleted, yielding its nutrients to plants, and unless it is constantly replaced the soil dies. The soil lives as long as the recycling process is not interfered with – but interference is precisely what happens in a garden. We do not return everything to the soil. We may remove weeds to the compost heap, but we eat the crops we grow and send our wastes elsewhere. We cut flowers and throw them in the rubbish; we burn prunings; and in doing so, we diminish the humus supply. We may even add poisonous chemicals that kill the micro-organisms. Clearly, we need to work to restore the balance.

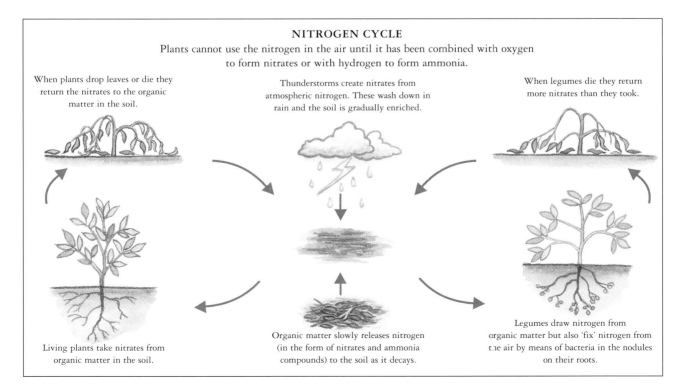

NITROGEN CYCLE

Plants cannot use the nitrogen in the air until it has been combined with oxygen to form nitrates or with hydrogen to form ammonia.

When plants drop leaves or die they return the nitrates to the organic matter in the soil.

Thunderstorms create nitrates from atmospheric nitrogen. These wash down in rain and the soil is gradually enriched.

When legumes die they return more nitrates than they took.

Living plants take nitrates from organic matter in the soil.

Organic matter slowly releases nitrogen (in the form of nitrates and ammonia compounds) to the soil as it decays.

Legumes draw nitrogen from organic matter but also 'fix' nitrogen from the air by means of bacteria in the nodules on their roots.

MAINTAINING A
HEALTHY SOIL

ORGANIC GARDENING AIMS TO FEED THE SOIL WITH NATURAL MATERIALS
TO CREATE THE BEST ENVIRONMENT FOR HEALTHY PLANT GROWTH

A fundamental principle of organic gardening is the creation and maintenance of a healthy soil, one that has a good structure, aeration and drainage, is rich in available plant foods and is full of living organisms. This diverse range of creatures, from fungi to earthworms, will help to maintain a natural balance and provide the best conditions for healthy plant growth.

ORGANIC MATTER

Unless the organic matter from which the humus is continually being created is replenished, the soil will gradually die. It is no good bypassing the natural process of creating humus by adding chemical fertilizers: they may boost the growth of plants for a little while, but they do not nourish the living creatures of the soil or create humus.

Chemical fertilizers can create other problems as well. When nutrients are so readily available, plants may take up so many that they will produce lots of soft, sappy growth which is particularly susceptible to attack by pests and diseases. To make the fertilizers soluble, they contain all sorts of

things the garden does not need. Sulphate of ammonia yields nitrogen from the ammonia, but the sulphate part poisons worms, bacteria and fungi. And their very solubility means that any nutrients the plants do not take up at once wash away with the rain, to pollute the ground water and eventually rivers, lakes, even the sea, with consequences that are all too familiar by now.

The orthodox gardener will point out that it takes a whole truckload of compost to yield the same amount of nitrogen that comes in one single bag of artificial fertilizer. Although that may be so, it is comparable to saying that a vitamin pill is as nutritious as an orange.

Organic matter – that is, material that was once alive – must be added continually to feed the humus. And if organic gardening has a central, positive idea, this is it. Feed the living soil, and all else will be added.

How do you do that? First, by recycling as much organic matter as possible from the garden itself. Fallen leaves, unwanted weeds, cabbage stalks, spent flowers – nothing should be wasted. The compost heap is the heart of the organic garden.

But you will never have enough compost because not everything you take out can be returned to the garden. The answer is to bring in other organic matter from outside. Compost your vegetable scraps, or buy in manure, blood and bone and other organic materials. It might even be possible to intercept stuff that would otherwise have gone to waste, saving your neighbours from the trouble of burning fallen leaves or dumping the clippings from their lawn by carrying them off (with their permission, of course) to your compost heap.

But you must be careful that, by bringing in material to your garden from elsewhere, you are not robbing other environments and other soils to feed your own. Peat, for example, is a popular organic soil conditioner and a good one too; but peat is not a readily renewable resource and the bogs from which it is taken are rapidly being exhausted.

Composted wood waste makes just as good a mulch, and even a planting compost, as peat – and wood is a renewable resource.

ADDING ORGANIC MATTER

If you are preparing a new bed, for vegetables or for flowers, then spread the organic matter and fork it in to mix it with the soil. It is incorporated more quickly that way and the bed will be ready to plant all the sooner. Around established plants where you do not want to dig deep and disturb plant roots, spread it on the surface as mulch. As it decomposes it will filter down into the soil, and the worms will take it down with them. A more-or-less permanent mulch is a good idea. Not only does it keep the soil cool, it smothers weeds and conserves moisture. An organic mulch looks much better than bare soil, too.

It takes time to build humus, especially if it has been depleted by wasteful gardening and poisoned by the indiscriminate use of insecticides, fungicides and artificial fertilizers. It also takes time to get used to the idea of feeding the soil not plants. Patience, however, will be rewarded by ever more fertile soil – and an ever more abundant and rewarding garden.

No section of the garden makes more demands on the soil than does the vegetable garden, with its need for constant, luxuriant growth. This vegetable garden has been kept in full productivity for many years by regular applications of compost and manure.

SOIL CONDITIONERS AND FERTILIZERS

We will look at composts and manures on pages 64–75, but other materials will also improve the soil and supply useful minerals and trace elements.

• **Spent mushroom compost.** A useful mulch and soil conditioner, it will also supply some nutrients. It is made from strawy horse manure, peat and chalk or limestone that has been used to grow a mushroom crop. Unless it is from organic sources, stack it for at least six months before use to allow any pesticide residues to break down. Do not use on acid-loving plants because of the high pH.
• **Shredded bark.** A good soil conditioner and decorative mulch. Fine grade, partly composted and coarser grades are available. Best applied as a mulch rather than dug in as it can cause nitrogen deficiency.
• **Spent hops.** If you are able to obtain spent hops, they can be dug in to increase the organic matter. They also provide a small amount of nutrients.
• **Seaweed.** Very rich in plant foods, particularly potassium and trace elements, and an excellent soil conditioner as the alginates bind soil particles, improving soil structure, and stimulate bacterial action. Use fresh or add to the compost heap as an activator. Collect only from unpolluted beaches.
• **Rock potash.** A good source of potassium. This is not readily soluble and remains in the soil for a long time, so plants can take it up over a long period.
• **Wood ashes.** A useful supply of potassium and other minerals. They are soluble and easily leached out of the soil so apply them around growing plants.
• **Bonemeal.** A rich source of phosphorus, which is released slowly. It stimulates root growth. Buy only bonemeal that is steam-treated.
• **Blood, fish and bone.** Good general fertilizer that contains phosphorus, nitrogen and some potassium.
• **Dried blood.** A fast-acting nitrogen fertilizer and good compost activator.
• **Fish meal.** High in nitrogen and phosphorus. Check the label as some manufacturers add inorganic potash.

• **Seaweed meal.** Contains nitrogen, phosphorus and potassium and a full range of trace elements. Use to correct trace element deficiencies, as a compost activator and as a general fertilizer. It is more effective applied in warm weather as increased bacterial action will break it down more rapidly. Liquid seaweed products are very useful for correcting trace element deficiencies very rapidly.

ACIDITY AND ALKALINITY

Soil pH is a measure of the acidity/alkalinity of the soil. This affects the solubility of minerals and their availability to plants, the range of plants that will grow and the activity of various soil organisms, both beneficial and harmful. The pH range for good plant growth is generally between 5.5 and 7.5, but can vary for different types of plants. Beyond this range nutrients become less available, limiting the growth of many plants, and the activity of various soil organisms is affected. Earthworms will not thrive if the soil is too acid, while some pests and diseases such as club root and wireworms are more prevalent in acid soils. Others, like potato scab, occur more frequently on alkaline soils.

The pH of acid soils can be raised by the addition of ground limestone, dolomitic limestone or even calcified seaweed, but it should not be added at the same time as manure as they will react causing nitrogen to be lost as ammonia gas. Add plenty of compost and manure to alkaline soils every year and the alkalinity will gradually be reduced. Avoid liming or using comfrey manure or mushroom compost, which all make the soil more alkaline.

TO DIG OR NOT TO DIG?

At the heart of many gardeners' soil care routine is digging, but is it essential? Traditionally, digging has been a regular task to break up compacted soil, improve aeration and drainage, work in organic matter, expose soil pests to predators or the weather and dig in weeds. However, as well as being hard work, there are arguments to say that digging is not

FROM THE TOP • *Deep beds edged with planks provide a good, fertile soil for vegetable crops. Net provides protection from rabbits.* • *A compost heap is the heart of an organic garden; every gardener should be able to find room for one.* • *Flowers mingle attractively with vegetables in this potager-style vegetable garden. Narrow beds mean that most of the work can be done from the paths.*

essential and may even be detrimental. Potential problems are that it may damage soils, causing the natural soil structure to deteriorate and disturbing the soil organisms. It can also bring weed seeds to the surface where they will rapidly germinate.

It is possible to have a no-dig garden where mulches of compost, manure or other organic matter are added to the surface of cleared ground. Crops are planted through the mulch, which increases fertility, suppresses weeds and conserves moisture.

DEEP BEDS

Many organic gardeners use a system of deep beds for growing vegetables. In this simple and highly productive system little digging is done after the initial thorough cultivation.

The area is divided up into narrow beds separated by paths. The beds are made narrow enough that all work can be done from the paths and are generally no more than 1.2m (4ft) wide. If preferred, the beds can be edged and raised slightly. This helps improve the drainage, which is particularly valuable on heavy soils. The paths can be narrow, only 30cm (12in) wide to save space, but should be at least 60cm (24in) wide if a wheelbarrow is to be used.

The beds are initially dug deeply, and lots of organic matter incorporated, but from then on further digging is avoided. A deep mulch, such as well-rotted manure or compost, is added each year. Compaction is avoided as the beds are not walked on and a good soil structure with lots of earthworms and other soil organisms develops. The deeply worked, fertile soil, and the fact that there is no need to walk on the beds, means crops can be planted more closely, usually in blocks rather than rows. This makes optimum use of the space and results in much higher yields than from a conventional plot.

Another bonus is less weeding. As there is little disturbance to the surface of the bed, other than planting and harvesting, few weed seeds are exposed. This, together with close planting and regular mulching, makes it difficult for weeds to establish and means that less weeding is necessary.

MAKING YOUR OWN

COMPOST

THE COMPOST HEAP IS THE VERY HEART
OF AN ORGANIC GARDEN

THE IMPORTANCE OF COMPOST

There is something especially satisfying about making compost, starting with rubbish and ending up with this wonderful, almost good enough to eat stuff; dark, crumbly, sweet-smelling and the most potent soil improver there is. Its goodness comes from being full of humus, and humus is the most important thing of all in keeping soil fertile. It also contains the enzymes and vitamins that the soil micro-organisms need to thrive, and it is alive with micro-organisms. No gardener ever has enough compost, let alone too much, and no self-respecting garden should be without its compost heap.

There are people who believe that anything worthwhile is only won by trouble and suffering and like to give the impression that making compost is difficult, full of potential disasters. But compost is nothing but rotted organic matter. Gather enough of the right stuff together in a heap and it literally makes itself. All the various refinements and manipulations are really only to speed things up; if you are patient, you can be lazy.

MAKING COMPOST

The right stuff

In theory, compost can be made from anything that was once alive, but in practice some things are more practical to use than others. These include:

• **Kitchen rubbish.** Vegetable and fruit trimmings, tea leaves, coffee grounds and the like can be used, but be wary about too many citrus peelings and bits of pepper. Their pungency temporarily upsets worms.
• **Spent vegetable plants.** Left-overs of the plants in the vegetable garden can be used, once you have harvested the crops, as well as the trimmings off the vegetables from the shops. Chop brassica stems into small pieces, and avoid club-root infected plants. Avoid plant material that may contain persistent diseases such as blight or tobacco mosaic virus.
• **Leaves.** Leaves of plants such as comfrey and nettle are high in nutrients and make excellent additions to the compost heap, also acting as activators. Rhubarb leaves, though poisonous to eat, are safe to compost. Bracken leaves can be composted when green. Avoid them when they are producing

spores. Material from cutting back plants in the flower garden is useful as long as any diseased material and seedheads are avoided. A limited number of fallen leaves can also be added to a heap, but they are perhaps best used to make leaf mould or used as a mulch.

• **Grass clippings.** A source of quickly available nitrogen, they are the mainstay of many heaps, but try to mix them with other, coarser material, as a thick layer will get wet, exclude air and rot slowly.

• **Prunings.** Soft prunings and hedge clippings can be added directly to the heap, but woody prunings should be shredded or chopped up small, and only used in small quantities. Avoid thorny prunings. Conifer and evergreen cuttings will eventually break down but will tend to make an acid compost.

• **Green manure crops.** Bulky green manure crops, such as lupins or field beans, can be grown for adding to the compost heap. (See pages 73–4.)

• **Weeds.** In theory, compost heaps get hot enough to kill off pernicious weeds but do not chance it. Perennial weeds can contain a lot of nutrients, so make a valuable addition to the heap as long as they are killed first. Leave them in the sun to die and dry out before composting. Annuals can be added before they have set seed. Weed seeds will survive if the heap does not get hot enough, and you will be spreading weeds around the garden in the compost.

• **Manure.** 'Farmyard manure' based on straw adds nitrogen and enzymes to help the vegetable matter rot and enriches the final product. Fresh manure is best set aside for a few weeks to cool down, or used just in small quantities as a compost activator. Manure from horses kept on wood shavings can also be used, but more sparingly. Bedding from pets such as rabbits and guinea pigs can be added, but avoid adding dog and cat manures as they may contain organisms that are harmful to humans.

• **Straw.** This is useful to bulk up the heap. If it is dry, wet it before adding it to the heap.

• **Hay.** Even better than straw, as it contains more nutrients. Again, soak it well if it is dry.

• **Sawdust.** Although sawdust used on its own sets like cement, it can be included in small quantities

FROM TOP: *A plastic compost bin placed beside a path for easy access. The lilac-pink flowers are* Tulbaghia violacea.
• *The heap at the far end is ready for use; the autumn leaves, still fresh, will take at least a year to compost.* • *The ideal triple bin, with dividers of heavy planks supported by steel stakes.* • *Compost at its most basic — a heap under a tree. The self-sown poppies add a splash of colour.*

if mixed with other things to keep it open, but it needs a starter such as poultry manure.

• **Seaweed.** Collect seaweed from unpolluted beaches only. Contains potassium and trace elements and acts as an activator.

• **Ash.** Ash from burning wood (not coal), including prunings too big to compost, is a useful addition, providing potassium and lime.

• **Hair, feathers and fabric.** Hair and feathers contain nitrogen and small amounts can be used if mixed well with other materials. Fabric should be pure wool or cotton.

• **Fertilizer.** Left-over organic fertilizers such as bonemeal or blood and bone can be included.

• **Urine, human.** Small quantities well-diluted with water provide nitrogen and potassium.

The wrong stuff

What can you not put on the compost heap? There are some things that cause problems.

• **Meat scraps.** These will compost, but are best avoided if rats are likely to be a problem. If you do add them, bury them well or they will attract flies.

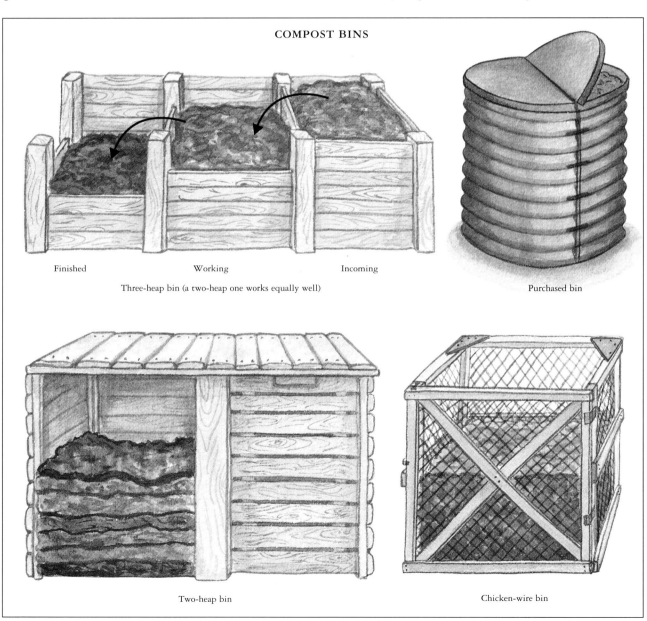

COMPOST BINS

Finished   Working   Incoming

Three-heap bin (a two-heap one works equally well)

Purchased bin

Two-heap bin

Chicken-wire bin

- **Oil.** Fried things or salad leftovers that have been dressed in oil are doubtful; the oil often sets like lacquer and preserves them.
- **Plastic, glass and metal.** These will not rot, naturally enough, but they do have a habit of sneaking unnoticed into the household rubbish.
- **Diseased plants.** Do not include plants affected by disease, such as club-rooted cabbages or black-spotted rose leaves. The heap might get hot enough to kill the disease organisms, but it is safer to burn them and add the ashes to the heap.
- **Paper.** This accounts for a large part of most people's rubbish. It is made from wood, but it does not rot easily unless you shred it and throw in something very rich in nitrogen, such as poultry manure. Then it is all right, newspaper especially (the paper used for glossy magazines rots very slowly), and it does help the texture of your heap, balancing by its dryness the sappy grass clippings and lettuce leaves. Avoid paper with coloured inks.

ACTIVATING THE HEAP

You can buy little boxes of 'compost starter' which contain appropriate bacteria and enzymes to get the rotting going, but if you include natural activators, such as young nettle or comfrey leaves, poultry manure, seaweed or urine, no additions should be necessary. Or you could throw on a bucket or two of finished compost from the last heap. Commercial activators based on bacteria or herbs are the most appropriate for the organic garden; avoid chemical activators based on nitrogen.

HOW TO MAKE THE HEAP

The first step when making a compost heap is to find a convenient place to put it. It should be accessible but out of the way – you may be proud of your prowess as a recycler and compost maker, but your dinner guests do not want to inspect the goings-on. The container is best sited on bare soil and ideally in a warm, sheltered spot. Make sure there is easy access and space to stack materials or turn the compost.

MAKING A BIN

An uncontained pile of compost tends to spread. It is better to keep it compact by putting it in a bin. A compost bin is just a bottomless box, usually of wood, big enough to hold about a cubic metre. Make two, side by side, the second bin to take new stuff while the first is full and maturing.

Some people like to give their compost bins a concrete floor to prevent nutrients washing out and roots getting in, but it also keeps worms out. Compost is thought to be better made in contact with the soil; micro-organisms as well as worms can come and go as they like, and rain can drain away, avoiding the need to put a tarpaulin over the heap to keep it from getting waterlogged. Yet another school of thought prefers to raise the compost above the ground on a slatted base so that air can get in from all sides and accelerate the rotting process.

FILLING THE BIN

The perfect way to fill your bin is to prepare all the layers at the same time – a 15cm (6in) layer of one material, then a sprinkling of activator, a layer of something else, more activator, and so on to the top, watering as you go if the raw material is dry, and then thatching the whole thing with a layer of straw. You need to use about a cubic metre of material to achieve a critical mass.

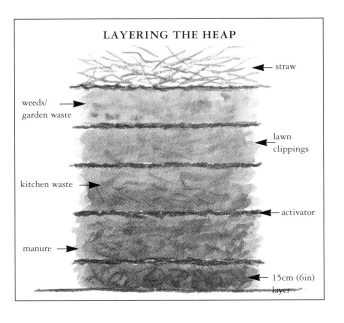

LAYERING THE HEAP

straw

weeds/ garden waste

lawn clippings

kitchen waste

activator

manure

15cm (6in) layer

ECONOMICAL COMPOST BIN

Turn a plastic garbage bin upside down, cut out the base and cut holes in the sides.

Maintaining a balance is important: too many fine, wet things and the heap will become a soggy mess that will putrefy rather than rot; too many dry, coarse ones and the process will take for ever.

The rotting process starts almost at once, and within days the heap heats up to the point where weeds and disease spores are killed. The outside of the heap does not get so hot — it loses heat to the air — so, after a period varying from a week to a month or so, you turn the heap inside out. This is heavy work; it may be enough simply to transfer the whole show into a second bin. Perfectionists turn a second time. Some two to six months after you started (the precise timing varies depending on factors such as temperature), you end up with a wonderful, weed-free, disease-free compost, with not an unrotted leaf or cabbage stalk in sight. It is ready when it is all black, just moist and crumbly.

ALTERNATIVE METHODS

The above is the classic method of making compost, but it is not always possible to do more than approximate it. To begin with, a cubic metre is more than most suburban gardens generate at one time. For many gardeners, the heap will have to be built up slowly: a wheelbarrow of lawn clippings, a bucket or so of kitchen scraps, a bag of prunings at a time. Which means that, even with the occasional addition of a layer of activator, the heap may never get hot enough to be certain of the destruction of all the weed seeds, and may take longer to work. If you have the space, stack the materials for a few weeks before building the heap. But whichever way you do it, try to follow the layer principle outlined above.

Turning the heap is also one of those jobs there never seems to be time for, with the result that there is always a quantity of not-quite-rotted stuff around the edges. No matter — it can finish rotting in the garden. Anything that looks as if it really needs more time in the heap can go into the second bin, which is started when the first is full.

Lazy compost like this takes longer (up to twelve months), but do you really need compost in two months? It is only the first heap that keeps you waiting; once you have your double heap up and running, there will always be compost to hand.

PLASTIC BINS AND TUMBLERS

In a very small garden, you can use one of the bottomless plastic compost bins that you find in most garden centres — they hold about two-thirds of

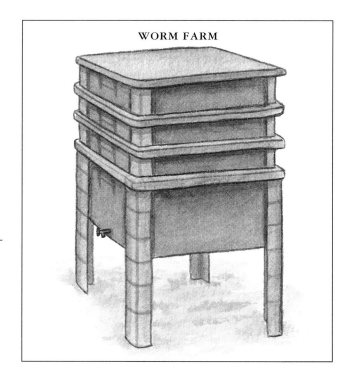

WORM FARM

a cubic metre – or even a plastic rubbish bin with the bottom cut out and a few holes in the side for ventilation. You can also buy containers mounted on a frame with a handle that enables the whole thing to be rotated by hand. It can be filled with the same sorts of material you would use in a conventional bin. After leaving it for a few days for composting to start, the bin should be rotated several times each day. Generally, compost tumblers heat up well, and the material composts rapidly, producing results after three weeks or so.

WORM FARMS

The idea behind worm farms is that you provide a home for worms and feed them kitchen scraps, which they turn into compost. Not so much compost, really, as worm manure, which is nearly as rich as poultry manure. You can improvise a worm farm out of a rubbish bin with the bottom cut out, but the ones you buy are more sophisticated, involving a series of tiers, the top one being where you put the scraps and the worms, the bottom one where you collect the compost; beneath that there is usually a bin where liquid manure accumulates, which can be diluted with water and used as a liquid feed.

WHAT CAN GO WRONG?

There is little that can go wrong with a compost heap. The most common problem is that the heap smells rotten. This means there is not enough air getting in and anaerobic bacteria, which can survive without oxygen, are at work. These bacteria, however, are not efficient compost makers. That is why the prudent compost maker always pokes a few holes in a new compost heap with a garden stake and does not get carried away with a great unventilated pile more than a metre high and wide – though the heap can be any length you wish. The whole mess may be waterlogged too.

The remedy is simple: take a garden stake and create one sharp end. Use this to stab the heap as deep as you can go in half a dozen places. That will let in air, and the smell should clear up promptly. If

LEFT: *A compost tumbler can produce small amounts of compost quite rapidly.* RIGHT: *A heap will not rot if it is too dry; if necessary, water the layers as you add them.*

the heap still stinks after a few days, you may need to turn the heap with a garden fork.

If the heap does not heat up, or starts to heat up then slows down, the answer is again to turn the heap, forking through it to incorporate more air. Add water if it looks dry, or dry material if it looks wet, before re-stacking the heap.

HOW GOOD A FERTILIZER IS COMPOST?

Just how good a fertilizer compost makes depends on how you measure it. By the standards of an artificial fertilizer, the amounts of available nitrogen, potassium and phosphorus (the NPK figures) are rather low and variable as compost is not a nicely standardized product. It is not the sort of fertilizer that forces an instant spurt of growth; its benefit is the long-term one of enriching the soil, improving both its structure and its overall fertility.

However, if your soil is naturally low in one particular element, the plants you grow on it and hence your compost will be short of it, too. This is an easy problem to overcome. Simply add the required elements to the heap, preferably in a form on which the micro-organisms can work. Anything rich in protein – blood, fish and bone, manure – will add nitrogen; bonemeal supplies phosphorus; potash comes from wood ash or seaweed. Seaweed will also provide a range of trace elements that plants need.

MAKING THE MOST OF
MANURE

GOOD QUALITY MANURE IS THE BEST
OF ALL FERTILIZERS

Manure has now become something of a luxury for the gardener. Until surprisingly recently, almost everyone who could afford to keep a garden also kept a horse, which gave a constant supply of free manure, to be heaped up in a pile and bestowed on the garden when it was nice and rotted. And it was bestowed with a lavish hand – old gardening books are full of such directions as 'mulch the rose beds four inches deep with old, rotted manure'. That would break the household budget today.

These days, most of us buy our manure in bags at the garden centre, and the question has to be asked whether it is really value for money. On the face of it, no: the proportion of the big three nutrients that manure contains is rather low, and, pound for pound, artificial fertilizers give more nitrogen, phosphorus and potassium. But manure rots down to make humus to benefit the soil and its micro-life ultimately benefits your plants. Manure remains the best of all fertilizers, with compost running a close second. Chemicals, which ultimately impoverish the soil, are not even in the race.

The relatively low direct nutrient content of manure is why it was always used in such lavish quantities, but these days we simply use as much as we can afford. As with so many things, it is much cheaper to buy manure in bulk. A look through the classified advertisements in the local paper should turn up a source, but be prepared to take delivery by the tonne. (Not that a tonne goes all that far in anything other than the smallest garden.)

ALLOW IT TO COOL

If the manure you buy is fresh it will be far too strong and 'hot' to use. It creates a lot of heat as it ferments, and the manure will probably burn any soft leaves or roots that it touches. Leave it in a heap for six weeks or so; if you like, you can put a plastic sheet over it to keep the rain from leaching the nitrogen out. This also allows you to assess whether the manure contains a lot of weed seeds as they will germinate in this time. Those deep in the heap will probably be killed off by the heat of fermentation and any that come up on the surface can be put on the compost heap. If there is room in the bin you can add some of the manure to the compost heap, where it will act as an activator.

KINDS OF MANURE

The best sort of manure is the one you can get most readily and cheaply, but there is a traditional ranking order of richness.

• **Poultry manure** is the hottest, and the smelliest. It is so strong it needs to be used as sparingly as you might use an artificial fertilizer, and you might prefer to use it to enrich the compost heap (it is the best of all compost 'starters') rather than applying it directly to the garden.

Pelleted, dehydrated and more-or-less deodorized poultry manure is sold in bags and can be put straight on the garden beds to give plants a quick boost – but you should still be wary of allowing it to come in direct contact with the plants, as it can still burn. Store pelleted poultry manure under cover; if the rain gets to it, you will have a soggy and smelly mess.

• **Pigeon manure** is much the same as poultry, but you are unlikely to come across it unless you keep pigeons yourself. (It was for the manure as much as for pigeon pies that dovecotes were built in the past.)

• **Horse manure** ranks first among the dung of animals, which is all pretty much the same, and not nearly as rich as that of birds. Most horse manure we get these days is raked out from stables rather than collected from paddocks and is a mixture of half-rotted straw bedding wet with urine; it contains relatively little dung. It is the urine that burns, and horse manure must be heaped and cooled down before you can use it, or small quantities added to the compost heap. The nitrogen in the urine will not be lost: it will be put to use in rotting the straw.

These days many stables keep horses on wood shavings or sawdust. These are high in carbon, low in nitrogen and can rob soil of available nitrogen. Shavings can still be used, but try to find a source with a high proportion of urine and droppings in the shavings, and leave it to rot thoroughly for at least six months to a year. Mixing it with grass mowings and watering with urine can help it to rot.

• **Mushroom compost** is usually based on horse manure, and it makes excellent fertilizer when the crop of mushrooms is over. But though it is sold as 'spent' mushroom compost, it is sometimes still quite hot – if it comes out of the bag warm and smelling strongly of ammonia, it is best heaped up under cover for at least a couple of weeks.

Mushroom growers often add lime when making up their composts, so you should be wary of putting mushroom compost around lime-hating plants, such as camellias and azaleas. It may also contain pesticide residues, so in an organic garden it would be best to store it for at least six to twelve months before use to allow the residues to break down.

• **Cow and sheep manure** are next best, with goat manure close behind. Again, they are best heaped for a month or so before use. As with mushroom compost, let the warmth and smell be your guide. Cow manure is normally fairly moist and crumbly, sheep manure tends to be dry, almost like lumps of brown plaster. Dig it in rather than use it as mulch.

• **Pig manure** is the 'coldest' of all, and needs the shortest composting time, but in many countries it is unavailable for health reasons. However, if pigs are properly kept their manure should pose no danger to people.

Fresh manure can be too 'hot' to use immediately – stack for a few weeks or months before spreading or digging in. A small amount of fresh manure makes an excellent compost activator.

LEFT: *Sheep manure is high in nutrients and is worth collecting from the fields. Small amounts can be used to make liquid manure.*
RIGHT: *Ordinary plastic dustbins are a practical way to store and carry scraps from the garden or kitchen, or small amounts of manure.*

• **Caution.** Unless you are able to get your manure from an organic source, it is very likely to contain significant chemical residues. Do not use manure from non-organic sources immediately. Leave it for at least six months to allow the chemical residues to break down. Manure from intensive farms, such as battery hen houses, should not be used at all as the levels of chemicals, such as antibiotics and growth promoters, are likely to be very high.

USING MANURE

Once mellowed, manure offers two choices for applying it to the garden: it can be dug into the soil or spread as a mulch. One is not better than the other, and both can be done, digging it in to enrich the soil before planting (ideally a couple of weeks before, to allow the soil micro-organisms to get used to its presence), and spreading it as a mulch on established beds of perennials or roses.

Manure, like compost, acts slowly in releasing its nutrients, especially in winter when the nutrient-releasing bacteria in the soil are sluggish with the cold. This means you can put down the mulch, or dig in the manure at any convenient time, knowing that its goodness will be held in readiness until the weather warms up and the plants start looking for it. It is impossible to do the same with chemical fertilizers. Unless you time your applications of those fertilizers carefully, at best they will be washed away and wasted, at worst they will force unseasonable growth which is liable to suffer from cold or any insects and diseases that may be about. Let your plants grow according to their own natural rhythms, and do not be impatient for instant results.

LIQUID MANURES

Although not a substitute for feeding the soil in true organic tradition, liquid feeds can be useful for container plants or for plants growing in a poor soil.

Homemade liquid feeds can be made from manure, as described in the panel opposite, collected from a worm compost bin, or made from the leaves of plants with a high nutrient content, such as comfrey.

Simply pack the leaves into a container and cover with water. A container with a lid should be used as all these liquids can be rather smelly. (So be careful where you site the container.) Any size can be used, from an old plastic drinks bottle to a large bin or water butt. A water butt style container, raised on bricks, is useful for larger quantities as the resulting liquid can then simply be drained off via the tap.

This liquid can be used for plants in containers and growbags, or in moderation for those growing on poor soils. Dilute it with water, if necessary, so that it is a pale straw colour. Add the remains of the rotted leaves to the compost heap.

• **Comfrey.** Russian comfrey is a vigorous, deep-rooting perennial that can be grown especially for cutting as composting material and as a compost activator, as well as for liquid manure. The leaves are high in minerals, especially potassium and nitrogen, and established plants can be cut up to four or five times a season. Comfrey manure can be particularly useful as a feed for tomatoes and peppers.

• **Borage.** Related to comfrey, this can also be used to produce a liquid feed that is high in nitrogen.

• **Nettles.** The ideal way of disposing of these weeds is to make a good general purpose liquid feed. Young spring leaves are best as they contain higher levels of nitogen, potassium and phosphate. The resulting liquid must be well-diluted.

Proprietary liquid feeds, including plant extracts, seaweed and fish emulsion, are also available from shops and garden centres. Check that the one you choose carries an organic symbol as some, such as seaweed, may have had chemical fertilizers added.

GREEN MANURES

The practice of growing plants to improve soil fertility is a valuable one in the organic garden. Green manuring is a system of growing crops as temporary ground cover, which are then either dug into the soil, where they decompose, improving soil structure and fertility directly, or added to the compost heap. Additionally, while they are growing they help to prevent soil erosion or nutrients leaching out of the soil and to suppress weed growth. Legumes can be particularly valuable green manure crops as they can convert nitrogen into a form that plants can take up.

Most green manure crops are grown over winter on land that would otherwise be bare, but they can also be grown during summer, on bare land or as an undersowing beneath tall crops, such as sweet corn. The plants should not be allowed to set seed. Dig in the crop several weeks before you want to use the land. Short, sappy foliage can be dug in directly; bulky material should be cut, chopped if necessary, and allowed to wilt first, or the top growth put on the compost heap and the roots dug in.

MANURE WATER

There will be times when you want to give plants a quick boost: some vegetables as they come into bearing; annuals that need encouragement to go on for a few weeks longer; or the lawn when it is greening up after a period of drought. Then you can make manure water.

Put a couple of shovelfuls of manure (fresh will be all right) into a hessian bag and then steep it like an outsize teabag in a garbage bin full of water for a day or two until the water is the colour of weak tea. Then water your plants with it. Do not use it on dry soil, however, as it may be too concentrated. Keep the lid on the garbage bin; the brew smells and will attract flies. It will keep for a week or so, or you can pour any leftovers on the compost heap along with the contents of the used 'teabag'.

COMMON GREEN MANURES

• **Alfalfa.** A deep-rooting member of the clover family, alfalfa takes up and accumulates many nutrients, making it an excellent composting material. Sow in spring to dig in in autumn, or in summer for overwintering.

• **Buckwheat.** Fast-growing and producing plenty of organic material for digging in, this deep-rooting plant is excellent for improving soil structure. Its flowers are attractive to hoverflies and other beneficial insects. Frost tender, it can be sown in late spring or summer and dug in after two to three months.

• **Clovers.** Both annual crimson clover and perennial Essex red clover are widely used as green manures. If allowed to flower these legumes will attract bees and other beneficial insects. Do not grow on the same land for extended periods as the ground can get 'clover sick' from the exudates from the roots.

• **Fenugreek.** A fast growing green manure, this legume is a good catch crop between other summer crops. Frost tender, it can be sown from spring to summer, to be dug in within two to three months.

• **Grazing rye.** A cereal rye, not rye grass, this is excellent for overwintering, or for a rapid crop in early spring. It is a good soil improver and a good weed suppressor.

• **Lupin.** Although ordinary garden lupins can be used, agricultural lupins (*L. angustifolius*) make the best green manure. They are deep-rooting legumes that will improve the soil structure and produce plenty of bulky organic matter for the compost heap.

• **Mustard.** A fast-growing and widely used green manure; sown from spring to late summer it will produce plenty of organic material for digging in in eight to ten weeks. Related to the brassicas, it is susceptible to club root, and should be fitted in with the crop rotation if used in the vegetable garden.

• **Phacelia.** A delicate-looking plant that produces lots of attractive blue flowers that are much loved by bees and hoverflies; it can also produce a good quantity of material for composting. Grow for a couple of months in spring or summer, or try a late sowing – it will overwinter in a mild year.

• **Trefoil.** A low-growing legume, preferring light, limy soils, it is tolerant of shading and can be used for under-sowing. Sown in spring or summer, it can be left to overwinter if required.

• **Winter field beans.** One of the most commonly used of the peas and beans, this hardy annual is a good crop for heavy land. The top growth can be removed for composting and the roots, with their nitrogen-fixing nodules, dug into the soil. Bear in mind that they should not be used in the vegetable garden without considering crop rotation.

• **Winter tares.** These legumes will overwinter from a late summer sowing, or can be grown through spring and summer. Excellent nitrogen fixers, they also produce lots of useful bulk material for composting.

The above are a selection of commonly-grown green manure crops. From left to right: alfafa, lupins and Phacelia. *All three can be grown as temporary ground cover, then dug into the soil, where they decompose, or added to the compost heap.*

KEEPING WEEDS DOWN

Weeding is like housework. Nobody likes it, but here are some tips on how to minimize the chore.

• **Plant generously.** One of the most effective methods to combat weeds is to plant generously with your chosen plants: bare earth is an invitation to weeds. Bear in mind though that close planting has its limitations, particularly in the vegetable garden – you do not want tomatoes crowding each other for light and air, setting themselves up for fungal diseases, for example. Green manures can be used between crops in the vegetable garden, rather than leaving the ground bare.

• **Use mulches.** Cover any bare earth between plants with mulch. A mulch is a layer of material to cover the ground which excludes light, smothers weeds, conserves moisture and keeps the soil temperature even. It protects the surface from caking like a mud pie under the impact of rain and watering. The odd weed will still come up, but it will be much easier to pull up out of the crumbly surface of a mulch than from the soil itself.

Compost and other organic materials are the best of all mulching materials as they are also soil improvers, but inorganic mulches such as gravel or shale are effective weed smotherers and moisture conservers, even if they do not add humus. Their use is limited to places where you are not planning to do any digging. It is, however, no use putting a mulch where weeds are already growing; they will just come up through it and thank you for the extra humus. You need to remove them first.

• **Hoe regularly.** Regular hoeing removes any weeds from the garden as soon as they appear, without giving them time to become established and to spread – plus it requires much less effort to remove small seedlings than established weeds. Try to hoe in dry, sunny weather as some weeds may re-root in moist conditions.

• **Dig out deep-rooting perennial weeds.** Remove as many of the roots as possible and keep hoeing to prevent any more establishing. With problem weeds, the creeping, spreading ones which re-root from the smallest scrap, dig out every bit you can find and put down a light-excluding mulch for at least a season, preferably two.

• **Put in physical barriers.** To help prevent creeping weeds spreading into your garden from adjoining ground, sink a physical barrier 15–30cm (6–12in) deep. Try heavy duty polythene, planks, metal sheets or breeze blocks.

• **Be vigilant.** Whatever method you use, by checking your garden frequently and removing weeds before they have a chance to become established, you will find the task much easier. It is especially important to remove any weeds before they have a chance to flower and set seed as many will spread with extraordinary rapidity if they are allowed to seed.

ABOVE: *A thick mulch applied to the bare earth between plants can help to suppress weeds and will save you a lot of work in the garden.*
LEFT: *However, in some areas there is no substitute for regular hoeing to remove weeds as soon as they appear, before they have time to establish.*

WATERING

AND SAVING WATER

WATER IS AN ESSENTIAL RESOURCE
THAT SHOULD NOT BE WASTED

Water is a natural resource and should not be squandered, as the recent increase in droughts and hosepipe bans have demonstrated. Appropriate watering is also an essential factor in maintaining healthy plant growth. Insufficient water will reduce growth and put plants under stress, making them more vulnerable to attack by pests and diseases, even before they reach the stage of wilting. Too much water can result in lots of leafy growth at the expense of crops or flowers, it can also leach nutrients from the soil and make the plants more vulnerable to various pests and diseases.

Although some plants, such as vegetables and summer annuals, have to be watered, in the ornamental garden it is a good idea to concentrate on plants that will grow with no more water than your local rainfall, and possibly to restrict the use of container plants which rely on daily watering.

Thrift in the use of water, as in other departments of life, does not mean meanness. Certainly, you water only when plants need it, but when you water, water generously and thoroughly. It is better to harden your heart and not water at all than to waste water giving plants a light pick-me-up with

the sprinkler. That only encourages the roots to stay close to the surface where they suffer as soon as the soil dries out again. It is much better to water deeply, allowing the surface to dry out between waterings in order to encourage the roots to go deep where the soil dries out less quickly. It is also helpful to group plants with similar water requirements, which allows you to water without waste.

WHEN TO WATER

With practice, you can learn to recognize when a plant actually needs some water. Long before they actually wilt, leaves and flowers begin to lose lustre and stiffness, grass loses its spring and shows your footprints when you walk on it. Some plants wilt much sooner than others – hydrangeas and sweet peas, for instance – though you need to interpret this with care: other plants nearby may not be suffering nearly so much.

Crops often benefit from extra watering at certain stages of growth. For example, watering when fruit and vegetables are forming and beginning to swell will give a better crop.

Do not water in the heat of the day if you can help it: much of your water will be lost to evaporation at once. It is better to wait for the cool of the evening, unless plants are actually wilting. Alternatively, water in early morning, so foliage can dry off during the day, minimizing the risk of mildews or fungi.

There are many ways of getting water on to the garden. The traditional watering can enables you to get the water exactly where it is needed, but is not practical for large areas. A hose or sprinkler system covers a larger area, but is wasteful and wets foliage which can be a problem in some circumstances. The most useful and economical system is a seep hose, laid between the plants, preferably under a mulch. Water is delivered direct to the plants' roots, without wastage from evaporation or from watering areas between the plants that do not require it.

With the increasing problems of drought over recent years, water storage systems are becoming an even more valuable consideration in the garden. It is a simple matter to position water butts to collect

Use water butts to collect rainwater from the house roof and from garden structures such as the greenhouse.

rainwater, and this water is better for the plants than treated tap water.

'Grey water' from sinks, showers and baths can also be collected for use on the garden in times of drought. Be careful only to use water that is not contaminated with chemicals; water from dishwashers and washing machines contains too many chemicals to be used safely on plants.

WAYS TO SAVE WATER

• **Select appropriate plants.** Where necessary, choose plants that will survive in your garden with only minimal watering.

• **Group plants that require similar amounts of water together.** Then you will not be wasting water on drought-tolerant plants growing amongst those that have a higher water requirement. Concentrate thirstier favourites where they will have most impact, such as near the front door.

• **Increase the organic matter in your soil.** This significantly increases its water-holding capacity.

• **Provide shelter from wind.** Wind dries out the garden as efficiently as it does the washing on the line and so make sure your garden is adequately sheltered, with fences or windbreaks of drought-tolerant trees and shrubs.

• **Reduce lawns.** Keeping lawns green through the summer can take a large amount of water. Could some be replaced with paving, gravel, decking or less thirsty ground-cover plants?

• **Use mulches.** Mulches help to conserve water by reducing evaporation. They moderate soil temperature too, as well as suppressing weeds. Gravel will do the job well, but organic mulches – such as compost, straw, fallen leaves or shredded bark – have the extra benefit of adding humus as they break down. Apply them when the soil is moist.

• **Keep weeds down.** Mulches help keep down weeds, and keeping your garden weed-free is one of the most important things you can do to save water. Weeds simply guzzle it (which is why they grow like weeds!) and it is not merely wasteful, it is folly to lavish water on plants you do not even want.

CONTROLLING
PESTS AND DISEASES

PESTS AND DISEASES CAN MAKE LIFE DIFFICULT FOR ANY
GARDENER BUT THEY CAN BE CONTROLLED ORGANICALLY

THE PROBLEM-FREE GARDEN

A catalogue of all the bugs and diseases that might attack your plants makes scary reading, that of the prescribed insecticides and fungicides even more so. But take heart: bugs are part of the natural order and few are as bad as they sound. Concentrate on keeping your plants thriving and you will have little need for all those poisons. You will never be able to remove every pest and disease, but the key in an organic garden is to create a balanced environment with healthy plants and beneficial wildlife which will keep the pests and diseases at a level where they will do little damage.

• **Build a healthy soil.** Plant health starts with the soil. If the soil is healthy, with lots of humus and the micro-organisms, the plants will be healthy and should be able to shake off pests with little assistance. Any organic gardener will vouch for the idea that a plant hurried along with artificial fertilizers will not be as able to shake off pests as well as one flourishing unforced in good soil.

• **Choose healthy, trouble-free plants.** Buy only healthy, strong-growing plants for your garden. Avoid those that are pot-bound, drawn and leggy or showing any signs of pest, disease or mineral deficiency. If possible, buy only certified virus-free seed potatoes, fruit trees or soft fruit.

The wise gardener concentrates on species that do not have a long list of ailments. Why turn the garden into a hospice for invalids when there are so many robust and desirable plants that will flourish without the spray gun? This is especially important with the plants that form the bones of your garden design: the trees, shrubs, hedges and ground covers.

Whatever the role a plant has in your garden, there is almost always a trouble-free plant that will play it. But remember, grow only plants that are suited to the conditions; even the most trouble-free plant will be apt to suffer if you grow it in a soil, climate or garden position that does not suit it.

• **Grow resistant varieties.** Choose resistant cultivars where they are available to lessen problems with pests and diseases. Plant breeders are continually trying to breed new resistant varieties, so consult the latest plant catalogues to find out what is currently available.

• **Practise good husbandry.** Keep your plants growing well to avoid any checks to growth that could weaken them and allow pests or diseases to establish. Well-prepared soil, with appropriate feeding and watering, is essential.

As well as growing each plant in suitable conditions, try to create a diverse planting in your garden. Growing lots of the same plant together creates conditions for pests and diseases to spread rapidly. A mixed planting avoids this problem, encourages a better ecological balance and a diverse community of wildlife, with beneficial creatures to keep the pests in check. Mix flowers, fruit, vegetables and herbs where it is practical, rotate crops to reduce chances of pests becoming established, and try companion planting. Protective barriers and traps, either physical or biological, can help protect against some pests.

• **Encourage beneficial wildlife.** In an organic garden, one of the major keys to pest and disease control is to create a balanced environment in which natural predators will thrive. As well as creating a diverse planting rather than a series of monocultures, you can take specific steps to encourage wildlife by providing them with food, water and shelter, and by avoiding using any sprays that will harm them. Insects such as hoverflies, lacewings and ladybirds will devour aphids, and larger creatures such as frogs, hedgehogs and birds will eat many pests such as slugs and snails, woodlice, millipedes and wireworms; even spiders are gardeners' friends, trapping and eating large numbers of flying pests.

• **Be vigilant.** Keep a regular look out for pests and diseases, so that you spot the first signs of trouble. Problems are much more easily dealt with if caught early, before they have a chance to get well established. For example, a leaf showing signs of mildew can be picked off, and a few aphids are easily pinched off between finger and thumb. If necessary, changes in watering or feeding regimes can also be made.

Birds provide a great service in the garden by eating prodigious numbers of insects, but they like to eat fruit, too. Netting the fruit as ripeness approaches is the best way to keep the birds off. Chicken wire is fine but cumbersome; the nylon mesh used by grape growers is more expensive but is much easier to handle. Alternatively, you can make a cage to keep the birds out, as we see on the left.

PESTS

ANIMAL PESTS

Animal pests range from humans to dogs and cats, mice and rabbits and so on. The best way to avoid human damage is to plan carefully. Make sure paths are wide enough and allow space for games and other activities. Barriers such as fencing are the best solution for rabbits and deer; mice and moles may need to be trapped if they become a severe problem.

Chemical or ultrasound cat and dog repellents are available. Cats usually sniff the ground before scratching, and a sprinkling of cayenne pepper around seedlings and seeds can keep them off. The concentrated urine that dogs and tomcats use to mark their territories will kill anything green it touches unless you can hose it off at once.

SLUGS AND SNAILS

These are a universal pest and it seems there is practically nothing that they will not eat. They especially love vegetables, newly planted seedlings and tender young shoots, and they can literally destroy a young plant overnight. Commercial snail

baits are usually based on metaldehyde, and are not appropriate in organic gardens. They are effective, but the snail takes time to die and in the meantime may be eaten by birds or other wildlife.

It is much safer to catch the snails and squash them, in the meantime protecting plants with a barrier of soot, coarse grit or lime, and encouraging natural predators such as hedgehogs, frogs and birds. Snails operate at night or while it is raining and you can hunt them with a flashlight, but setting traps is easier. The old standard is a saucer of beer: snails adore beer and in their greed will drown. Half-shells of orange or grapefruit are effective too; the snails will crawl inside during the night and can be removed in the morning. The snails will not be dead, so you will need to squash them. A biological control agent for slugs is now available in the form

CLOCKWISE, FROM ABOVE: *A plastic bottle baited with beer makes a good snail trap.* • *The artificial butterflies deter real cabbage butterflies.* • *Yellow objects attract many flying insects, and sticky yellow paper makes an effective trap.* • *A tube cut from a plastic bottle is a greenhouse for a tomato seedling — and it helps to keep the snails away.*

This trap, filled with beer, is even more attractive to slugs and snails than the tender young lettuce leaves.

of a microscopic nematode, *Phasmarhabditis hermaphrodita,* which will control slugs for up to six weeks. Other creatures that might eat the dead slugs are not harmed.

INSECT PESTS

Insects come in many varieties, and the first thing to ask when you see them is whether they are actually eating the plants. Some are carnivorous and prey on vegetarian insects; ladybirds and hoverflies being the best-known examples. If you decide they are doing harm, try to squash them. By catching the invasion early, you may avoid having to use an insecticide. All insecticides are poisons, so use with care and do not use on a routine basis, only as a last resort to prevent a particular pest getting out of hand.

The newer chemical insecticides are safer than some of the older brands, as they are less toxic and they do not persist in the environment for as long. But there is always a risk of unforeseen harmful effects, and of resistance building up.

ORGANIC PESTICIDES

Happily, there is a class of insecticides you can use with reasonable safety: those derived from plants, the 'botanical insecticides'. These are biodegradable and so they do not remain to pollute the environment, and as they are not just one chemical but a mix, there is less likelihood of insects developing resistance.

None of these insecticides persists for as long as chemical insecticides, and it does mean you may need to spray more than once. All sprays, 'safe' or not, should be treated as dangerous, stored out of harm's way and used on a windless day when they will not drift to areas where they are not wanted. The gardener should wear protective clothing while spraying and wash thoroughly immediately the job is done. Spraying in the evening, when beneficial insects are less active, is generally recommended.

In the past organic gardeners used to make home-made pesticides from rhubarb leaves, herbs and tobacco, but this is now illegal. All materials used as pesticides must have been registered as such.

PYRETHRUM

Derived from the flowers of the African chrysanthemum *(Chrysanthemum cinerariaefolium),* this is one of the safest insecticides and is the usual active ingredient in fly sprays designed for use indoors. It is most effective against small insects such as aphids, thrips or whitefly. Be careful when spraying near ponds as it is poisonous to fish. It can also harm some beneficial insects.

DERRIS

Derris, or rotenone, is a contact insecticide made from an extract of the roots of a tropical vine, *Derris elliptica.* It is a broad-spectrum insecticide, killing a wide range of pests, such as ants, aphids, beetles, caterpillars, earwigs, mites, thrips and weevils, but it will also kill beneficial insects. It lasts longer than pyrethrum too, about 48 hours, as opposed to 12–24 hours for pyrethrum. Use it in the evening, where practical, to minimize potential problems. Use with care near ponds as it is very harmful to fish.

SOFT SOAP

A soap of vegetable origin, soft soap is traditionally used as a treatment for aphids and red spider mites. You might like to add a little soft soap to other insecticides: it is a good wetting agent and helps them stick to the plant and to the bugs. Do not use detergent, however, as it is a great polluter.

INSECTICIDAL SOAP

Insecticidal soap is a potassium-salt soap that is more effective than soft soap in controlling pests such as aphids, red spider mites, scale insects and whitefly. It is non-persistent and is a contact insecticide so must actually reach the pests. It is useful for spot spraying where biological controls have been introduced.

BIOLOGICAL CONTROLS

As well as encouraging natural predators to your garden, there is an increasing range of 'biological controls' available. You can buy ladybirds to eat aphids, parasitic wasps to eat whitefly larvae and predatory mites to eat red spider mites. Most are suitable for greenhouse use, but there are some, such as *Bacillus thuringiensis* which is used to control caterpillars, that can be used on outdoor crops.

Most biological controls have a limited shelf-life and should only be ordered (usually by mail order) when needed. They need a certain temperature range in order to work effectively, so check the requirements before ordering, and they can be harmed by certain pesticides, so do not use if you have used the pesticides in the previous ten weeks.

BARRIER METHODS

Some pests can be kept away from plants very simply by means of physical barriers. Horticultural fleece or fine plastic mesh materials can be used to cover crops and protect them from pests such as carrot root fly and flea beetles, while still allowing light, air and rain to penetrate. The fleece will also give early crops added protection against frost. Other useful barriers range from simple cloches made from plastic bottles, to mats to protect brassicas from cabbage root fly and grease bands around fruit trees.

SOME COMMON INSECT PESTS
APHIDS

Aphids, including greenfly and blackfly, are one of the most widespread of garden pests and congregate on the soft shoots of many plants, from lilies to roses, from citrus to beans. Female aphids can breed without mating and numbers increase with amazing speed. They suck plant sap, causing distortion, weakening the plant, and sometimes killing it. They excrete sticky honeydew on which sooty mould fungus can grow, and can transmit virus diseases.

Inspect plants regularly as aphids need to be controlled at the first signs. A strong squirt from the hose will knock them senseless, and they rarely crawl back again, or you can squash them between your fingers. If you miss them and a plague builds up, pyrethrum, derris or insecticidal soap will despatch them most efficiently. Encourage natural predators, such as lacewings, ladybirds, hoverflies, spiders and bluetits. Companion plants such as French marigolds and poached egg plants will not only attract predators such as hoverflies but will also make a colourful display in the garden.

CATERPILLARS

These are common garden pests, the most widely affected group of plants generally being the brassicas, the leaves of which can be stripped by caterpillars of the cabbage white butterfly. Inspecting your plants regularly and removing caterpillars or eggs is the simplest means of control. Derris is as effective as traditional chemicals, and much safer, but should still be handled with caution. Even better is to use biological control, and spray the caterpillars with *Bacillus thuringiensis* – it is deadly to caterpillars, but not to birds that might eat them, and not to people. It is non-persistent, so you need to spray carefully to reach all the caterpillars and a later invasion of pests will require a fresh spray.

EARWIGS

Chrysanthemums, dahlias and other ornamental flowers are particular favourites of earwigs, and they make ragged holes in the petals, damaging the flowers. Smear grease on the stems, just below the flowers, to keep them away. Earwigs are easy to trap; simply fill a flower pot with straw or dried grass and put it upside down on top of a cane. The earwigs will crawl inside to avoid daylight and can be collected up and removed.

LEATHERJACKETS

Leatherjackets are the fat, greyish-brown larvae of the crane fly. They feed on plant roots and can be a problem in lawns. They are large – up to 5cm (2in) long – and are easily spotted in borders. In lawns, cover wet grass with black plastic or cardboard overnight. This should bring the larvae to the surface where they can be removed.

RED SPIDER MITE

These tiny mites are barely visible to the naked eye, and can build up to quite a severe problem before their presence becomes apparent. They suck plant sap, causing leaves to become yellow and mottled and eventually to drop off. The problem is worst in dry conditions, so mist the plants regularly. Severe infections can be treated with derris. A biological control is also available for use in the greenhouse, where the problem can be most severe. This is in the form of a tiny predatory mite, *Phytoseiulus persimilis*, which will eat the red spider mites.

SCALE INSECTS

These small creatures attach themselves, limpet-like, to the stems and leaves of plants, looking rather like small raised blisters, and therefore often going unnoticed in the early stages. They suck the plant's sap, producing honeydew on which sooty moulds can grow. Affected plants are weakened, their leaves yellowing and dropping off. Scale insects can be hard to treat because the scales protect them against sprays. It should be possible to scrape off the scales on some plants, and spraying with insecticidal soap or derris can help control them in the juvenile stage.

VINE WEEVILS

Vine weevil larvae eat the roots of many plants and can do a lot of damage, particularly to container plants. Plants wilt suddenly and do not recover when watered. If the soil is examined, fat larvae about 1cm (¹/₂in) long with white bodies and brown heads can be seen. Destroy any that are found, or make up a solution of derris and immerse the pot in it. A biological control, the nematode *Heterorhabditits megidis,* can be watered on to pots where vine weevil is suspected. It is most effective when the soil is warm, in late summer or early autumn.

WHITEFLY

Whitefly tend to hide under the leaves, but if you disturb them they fly up in a cloud of tiny white

Barrier methods can provide an effective deterrent to many insect pests. FROM LEFT TO RIGHT: *Fleece can provide a simple barrier, preventing the pests reaching the plants.* • *A mat placed around the stems of brassicas prevents the cabbage root fly laying its eggs in the soil around the roots.* • *A greaseband around the trunk will prevent winter moths reaching the leaves of fruit trees to lay their eggs.*

insects. They can be a pest both outdoors and in the greenhouse. They suck sap, weakening the plant, and sticky honeydew and sooty moulds may be present. If they become a problem in the garden, it may be necessary to spray regularly with derris or insecticidal soap. In the greenhouse other techniques can be used. Hang sticky yellow cards to trap them. If this is not sufficient to control the pest, the biological control *Encarsia formosa,* a wasp that parasitises the whitefly larvae, can be introduced.

WIREWORMS

A particular problem on newly cultivated ground, these thin, shiny beetle larvae feed on roots, stems and tubers of many plants, leaving characteristic small holes. Regular digging will expose the pest to predators, or pieces of potato, carrot or brassica stems can be used to trap wireworms. Lift the bait regularly, destroy the worms and replace with fresh bait.

OTHER INSECTS

There are various other insect pests, but just about all will succumb to botanical sprays. Just be sure before you squirt that they are actually doing harm.

DISEASES

BACTERIA

Fortunately, bacterial diseases of plants are fairly uncommon as they tend to be both serious and incurable. Symptoms include soft rot and cankers. If a problem strikes, all you can usually do is to burn the infected plant in case it spreads, and refrain from planting that plant in that spot for a couple of years.

VIRUSES

Plant viruses are very common. Many are not all that bothersome, for instance, striped tulips and camellias with white blotched flowers are virus-infected and they grow happily enough despite their illness. Rose mosaic sometimes causes yellow markings, like water stains, on rose leaves. It is more or less harmless – every plant of the super-vigorous 'Queen Elizabeth' in the world is affected.

Blackfly (left) *gather on the young shoots of broad beans. Remove by snipping off the shoots. The biological control,* Encarsia formosa, *can be used to control whitefly on tomatoes* (right).

There are, however, viruses that seriously weaken plants. Watch out for them as there is no cure; the only control is to destroy the infected plants. The best solution is to prevent infection in the first place.

Symptoms start with distorted and yellowish foliage and stunted growth, but sometimes all you see is a general decline in vigour. If you are offered certified virus-free stock of any plant, it is well worth paying the extra money for it. Do not save your own propagating material unless you are certain that the parent plants are clean.

Viruses are spread largely by other creatures such as eelworms and aphids. If aphids appear on a plant you know is virus-susceptible, deal with them promptly. And if you suspect a plant in your garden of having a virus, sterilize secateurs and the like after using them on it before you touch anything else with them. Chances are they will be carrying infected sap. A dip in neat bleach will do the job.

FUNGI

The fungi that live in humus are beneficial to the garden, those that attack living plants are not and they are a special problem for the organic gardener, as there are no 'safe' fungicides. Copper- and sulphur-based products are the most widely used in the organic garden, but copper and sulphur are both poisonous, and they accumulate in the environment, so their use should be kept to a minimum.

FUNGICIDES

There are several copper-based fungicides, including Bordeaux mixture, which is a mixture of copper sulphate and slaked lime and is widely used against diseases such as potato blight, and Burgundy mixture, which is a mix of copper sulphate and washing soda. They coat the leaves and remain active for up to several weeks.

Sulphur can be used against most fungi, including rust, powdery mildew and scab. It is sold as a dust or spray as a control and a preventive, but its use should be kept to the minimum. Some plants, especially varieties of top fruit and soft fruit, are 'sulphur-shy' and can be damaged by its application.

AVOIDING PROBLEM FUNGI

The only safe way to combat fungi is to watch the growing conditions: grow plants in healthy soil, do not overcrowd them and grow plants that are not susceptible. That is not too limiting as there are many plants that do not suffer from fungal diseases. Even among plants that do suffer, you can usually find cultivars and varieties with good disease resistance. It also depends a lot on climate: grapes, for example, are best adapted to a dry summer where mildew is only a minor nuisance, and humid summers can cripple them. Fortunately most fungi are more choosy about hosts than insects. If you get whitefly on beans, they will soon find the tomatoes, but your snapdragons could be orange with rust and the roses will be safe – rose rust is a different fungus.

LEFT: *Leaf spots are typified by the black spot so common on roses.*
RIGHT: *There are many types of rust, each affecting different plants. This is an example of leek rust.*

SOME COMMON FUNGI

MILDEWS

Mildews mainly attack leaves and are divided into powdery mildews, which cover leaves with a grey powder, almost always on the top, and downy mildews, which make a similar display on the undersides, with yellow or dead patches on top. Mildew is often a symptom of too little water at the roots and too much in the air and is worst if plants are crowded or shaded, so good husbandry is the most effective preventive. Remove and burn affected leaves. Sulphur is the traditional control.

RUST

Rust usually looks like its name: the leaves are covered in orange, yellow or brown raised pustules, almost always appearing first on the underside of leaves. The leaves eventually wither and fall. They are rather difficult to control and you should choose resistant cultivars where you can. All diseased plant material should be removed, and the rest of the plant can be sprayed with sulphur.

LEAF SPOT

Most leaf spots differ from mildews and rusts in that they get inside the leaf rather than just grow on the surface, and they are very difficult to deal with, being a particular problem in wet and humid conditions. Pick off affected leaves and burn them. The remaining plants can be sprayed with sulphur.

BOTRYTIS

Botrytis or grey mould thrives in cold, damp, crowded conditions, so the best preventive is good hygiene. Do not overcrowd plants, make sure greenhouse plants are well-ventilated, and avoid over watering and over-feeding. Cut out and burn infected shoots, and if necessary remove the entire plant.

HONEY FUNGUS

Honey fungus consumes the inner bark of the roots, killing them. It usually starts on a dead stump and then spreads to living plants. Remove and burn infected plants, and also the soil surrounding them.

COMPANION

PLANTING

The idea that some plants exert a beneficial effect on others growing nearby while some can exert an inhibitory influence is an ancient one that is now receiving renewed attention. Many of the ideas put forward have been used by gardeners for many years, sometimes for centuries, often derived from simple observation and common sense.

There are those who have dismissed the idea of companion planting as folklore and superstition, but there are in fact many good reasons why some plants can affect the growth of others. While research on specific planting combinations has so far given mixed results, there is obviously much more to be discovered and it is something well worth experimenting with in your garden.

The following are some examples of the ways plants can affect other plants growing around them.

Some plants release substances from their roots that affect surrounding life. Foxgloves (left) are said to release substances that stimulate the growth of plants around them, while French marigolds (right) release a compound that will kill nematodes.

ATTRACTING BENEFICIAL INSECTS

Beneficial insects include pollinators, which are particularly valuable for crop plants if they are to give a good yield, and those that are predators on the pests that damage garden plants. There are some plants that are particularly attractive to beneficial insects and these will make good companions for other garden plants. For example, both French marigolds *(Tagetes)* and pot marigold *(Calendula officinalis)* planted near tomatoes can reduce problems with aphids. This is because they attract large numbers of hoverflies, which are one of the best predators of aphids, consuming large numbers. Some plants attract a wide range of insects, while some are particularly good for bees or butterflies. Some of the best generally include the poached egg plant and morning glory. Choose a range of plants to flower over a long period for the greatest overall benefit for your garden.

DETERRING HARMFUL INSECTS

Perhaps the most classic example of companion planting is growing onions to deter carrot root fly. The smell of the onions disguises the smell of the carrots, which is what attracts the female flies to lay their eggs. Similarly, the cabbage white butterfly finds its host plant by smell, and planting French marigolds between the rows of cabbages confuses it and reduces the frequency of attack. In some cases, powerful odours can not only camouflage the plants but can drive insects away entirely, as is said to be the case with wormwood and related plants.

Visual camouflage can also be effective against pests. Some pests are attracted to particular plants by sight, and growing a mixture of plants with several different patterns and colours of leaves and flowers can make it difficult for the pests to find their host plants.

SACRIFICIAL AND TRAP PLANTS

Another way to use companion plants to reduce pest problems is to use 'sacrificial' or 'trap' plants.

This means growing plants that are particularly attractive to a problem pest, thereby attracting them away from the crop or flower that is to be protected. The sacrificial or trap plant, together with the pests that have gathered on it, can then be destroyed. For example, Chinese cabbage can be used to attract insects away from other brassicas, nasturtiums and basils can be used as trap plants for aphids, and mustard or potato for wireworms.

COMPETITION

In any environment there is a limited supply of the elements necessary to plant life – water, nutrients and light – and therefore there is inevitably competition for these resources. Plants that are most efficient at absorbing their requirements are more likely to succeed, often at the expense of others, perhaps shading them out or more efficiently taking up limited supplies of nutrients.

The best companion plants, therefore, are those that compete least with each other. Growing a deep-rooting plant with a shallow-rooting one means that they will be utilizing different levels of the soil, and thus reducing competition; growing a tall sun-loving plant with a shorter shade-loving plant means that they will both benefit from the conditions they require rather than competing with one another. Outdoor cucumbers, for example, are said to do particularly well in the light shade provided by a crop of sweet corn or sunflowers.

FROM LEFT: *Sweet corn grows well with beans and peas, and it is possible to grow climbing beans up the sweet corn plants.* • *Nasturtiums can be grown with courgettes or other squashes to help protect them from aphids and other bugs.* • *The poached egg flower,* Limnanthes douglasii, *is one of the best plants for attracting hoverflies, which are one of the best predators of aphids.*

AFFECTING THE PHYSICAL GROWING CONDITIONS

Different plants also have different degrees of tolerance to the conditions in which they are grown – sun and shade, moisture, wind and so on. A well-known example is clematis, which needs cool, moist conditions at its root. A companion planting of leafy ground cover plants will therefore encourage good growth. Similarly, tall-growing plants can provide shade for plants that do not do well in full sun, while wind-tolerant trees and shrubs can provide shelter for less tolerant plants, and fast-growing plants can act as 'nurse crops' for slower-growing or tender crops, as long as they are removed before they start to inhibit them.

IMPROVING SOIL CONDITIONS

The best-known of the soil improvers are the legumes, the pea and bean family. The bacteria in the nodules on their roots are capable of fixing nitrogen from the atmosphere, which will eventually become available in the soil for other plants. They are not only useful as green manures in preparing the ground for other plants, but will often increase the yields of other crops if grown amongst them.

There are some plants that are efficient mineral accumulators, absorbing minerals from deep layers of the soil or under conditions in which it is difficult for other plants to absorb them, and eventually making them available to other plants growing nearby. Many of the most efficient accumulators are weeds, so where you can, dig in or compost them to make the minerals available to your garden plants. For example, accumulators of iron include comfrey, beans, foxgloves, stinging nettles, chickweed and chicory; accumulators of sulphur, important for disease resistance, include members of the onion family, as well as purslane and horseradish.

Other plants can benefit the soil structure. Vigorous, deep-rooting plants can help break up heavy and compacted soils. Some plants, such as phacelia and flax, produce substances that bind together soil particles, and spinach is reported to produce compounds that improve the water-retaining capacity of the humus.

PRODUCTION OF BENEFICIAL OR HARMFUL SUBSTANCES

Many plants will release compounds into the soil around them, and these can either benefit or harm surrounding life. A classic example is the French marigold, which releases a compound which will kill nematodes, making it an excellent companion plant for crops that are susceptible to nematode damage. It has been reported that various plants, such as mustard and dandelions, can secrete chemicals which inhibit certain fungal diseases. Some plants, for example foxgloves, are thought to release chemicals that stimulate the growth or increase the health and disease resistance of nearby plants.

In contrast, some plants release compounds that inhibit the growth of plants around them, making them bad companions. Wormwood, for example, produces a toxic substance that inhibits the growth of nearby plants, and root secretions from buttercups inhibit the growth of clover. Clovers produce root exudates that inhibit other plants and eventually inhibit germination of their own seed, causing ground to become 'clover sick'. And it is not just root exudates that have an effect; for example, very few plants will grow under a walnut tree. Not only does the walnut cast deep shade: fallen leaves decay to form substances that kill off other plants.

Gaseous secretions can also be significant. Many plants release ethylene, which as well as hastening ripening can also inhibit seed germination and affect the growth rate of plants.

It can be hard to establish the degree of effect of these substances as they can be affected by all sorts of factors, including the weather, the time of year and soil conditions. On top of this, not all varieties and cultivars will necessarily produce the same effects. As with all aspects of companion planting, trial and error, to see what works in the conditions in your garden, may be necessary.

CLOCKWISE FROM THE TOP: • *Garlic is known for helping to reduce the problems of black spot on roses and to improve their perfume, though it is perhaps not as attractive for the job as the related chives. Garlic is a useful companion for many plants, discouraging aphids and other pests.* • *Tomatoes grow well with a companion planting of basil, and the two flavours complement each other as well.* • *French marigolds are an attractive addition to any vegetable garden, and are here seen growing with cucumber and basil. Cucumbers are also said to benefit from the light shade provided by tall plants such as sweet corn or sunflowers.*

GOOD COMPANIONS

These are some examples of plants that have long been regarded as good companions, and many gardeners have found them effective. Try them and see what happens.

- Basil with tomatoes, asparagus, beans, grapes, apricots and fuchsias – indeed with almost any other plant, except rue

- Beans with potatoes and sweet corn
- Borage with strawberries
- Chives with roses, carrots, grapes, tomatoes, fruit trees
- Cucumbers with sweet corn
- Garlic with roses, fruit trees
- Grapes with mulberries
- Horseradish with potatoes, almost any fruit tree
- Hyssop with cabbages, grapes
- Leeks with celery
- Lettuce with carrots, onions, strawberries
- Marigolds (French) with tomatoes, roses, potatoes, daffodils, beans
- Melons with sweet corn
- Mignonette with roses
- Mint with cabbages and other brassicas
- Nasturtiums with cucumbers, courgettes, squash, apple trees
- Onions with carrots
- Parsley with roses, asparagus, tomatoes
- Peas with carrots, turnips
- Potatoes with beans, cabbages, sweet corn, peas
- Sage with cabbages
- Sunflowers with squash, sweet corn
- Thyme with any brassica
- Tomatoes with asparagus, parsley, brassicas
- Wallflowers with apples

BAD COMPANIONS

Some of the unhelpful combinations to watch out for include:

- Apples with potatoes
- Beans and peas with garlic or onions
- Cabbages with strawberries
- Gladioli with strawberries, beans and peas
- Hyacinths with carnations
- Mint with parsley
- Beans with fennel
- Sunflowers with potatoes
- Tomatoes with potatoes, kohlrabi or fennel
- Wormwood with just about everything

A FINAL WORD

Organic gardening is a sane and sensible manner of gardening, and it works. The beautiful and productive gardens illustrated in this book are proof of that. But remember that organic gardening is an ideal – the emulation of Nature in the way it recycles all its organic matter through the soil to create ever-renewed life. The demands we make on our gardens, for fruit and vegetables, for cut flowers, and to create an attractive environment, put extra stresses on the natural balance. We need to work with Nature to maintain a healthy, balanced and diverse environment, but if we want more from our gardens than Nature unaided would give, we may need to compromise a little.

The sort of compromises you may have to make depends very much on the sort of garden you have. A big country garden can easily be self-sufficient in organic fertilizer, and control of pests and diseases is much easier where fields quarantine your garden plants from your neighbours'. In a suburban garden you have to give up some growing space to make room for compost and manure heaps, and you may find that your neighbours' neglected plants act as a source of infection for yours, making it more of a challenge to keep your garden pest- and disease-free.

The important thing is not to be obsessive. As long as you follow the ideal most of the time, you can feel happy with your efforts. Make compost – and if it runs out, buy not chemical fertilizers but manure. Learn to live with the odd bug. If a plague does mean resorting to the spray gun, then spray – but use only the least dangerous chemicals, and use only the minimum needed to do the job.

Most importantly, learn to look after the health of your soil, always replenishing its humus and avoiding as far as you can any chemicals that will interfere with its life. Nature will ensure that the garden that grows from it will burgeon in health and beauty. You will rediscover its eternal and harmonious rhythms and your garden will become a haven from our troubled and artificial world, both for you and for the wildlife that shares it with you.

I once had a sparrow alight on my shoulder for a moment while I was hoeing in a village garden, and I felt more distinguished by that circumstance than I should have been by any epaulet I could ever have worn.

Henry David Thoreau (1769–1862)

Flowers mingle in harmonious balance in this attractive organic garden. But there is more to organic gardening than the creation of a beautiful display such as this: by growing your own flowers, vegetables and fruit organically, you know that you will not be consuming harmful chemical residues along with your food.

INDEX

Page no.s in *italics* refer to illustrations

Published by Merehurst Limited, 2000
Ferry House, 51–57 Lacy Road, Putney, London, SW15 1PR

Text copyright © Merehurst Limited
Photography © Murdoch Books (except those listed below)

ISBN 1-85391-861 X

A catalogue of this book is available from the British Library.

COMMISSIONING EDITOR: Helen Griffin
SERIES EDITOR: Graham Strong
TEXT: Valerie Duncan
EDITORS: Rowena de Clermont-Tonnerre and Christine Eslick
DESIGN: Maggie Aldred and Wing Ping Tong
ILLUSTRATIONS: Sonya Naumov
PRODUCTION MANAGER: Lucy Byrne
PUBLISHING MANAGER: Fia Fornari
CEO & PUBLISHER: Anne Wilson
SALES AND MARKETING DIRECTOR: Kathryn Harvey
INTERNATIONAL SALES DIRECTOR: Kevin Lagden

Printed by Tien Wah Press in Singapore

PHOTOGRAPHS
All photographs by Lorna Rose © Murdoch Books except those by:
Malcolm Birkitt © Merehurst Limited: front cover, pp 2 (above left, above right, below left), 3 (above and below),
4 (left), 6 (left, right and below) 8 (left), 9 (above and below), 14, 15, 17 (left and right), 42 (left), 43 (right), 45,
47 (left and right), 49, 51 (right), 53 (above and below), 63 (above and centre), 69 (left and right), 71, 74 (left, centre
and right), 75 (above and below), 76 (right), 77, 81, 83 (left, centre and right), 84 (left), 85 (left and right),
86 (left), 87 (left, centre and right), 89 (above, below left and below right), 91; Valerie Duncan: pp 2 (above centre
and centre), 13, 17 (centre), 20 (left and right), 42 (centre and right), 44, 51 (left), 53 (centre), 76 (left and centre),
86 (right); Garden Picture Library: John Baker, p 63 (below); Mayer/Le Scanff, p 5; Ron Sutherland, p 6 (centre);
Denise Grieg: pp 50 (left), 84 (right); Andrew Lawson: p 7; Harry Smith Collection: p 8 (R)

ACKNOWLEDGEMENTS
The publishers would like to thank the Henry Doubleday Research Association
for kindly allowing photography to take place at Ryton Organic Gardens, Coventry
and at Yalding Organic Garden, Maidstone, Kent.

Front cover: A bright pot marigold creates a splash of colour in any garden
Title page: Figs ripening under the protection of chicken wire